CONFRONTING AMERICA'S HEALTH CARE CRISIS

Establishing a Clinic for the Medically Uninsured

Anne Boston Parish, MSN, RN, CS; FNP-C

authorHOUSE®

AuthorHouse™
1663 Liberty Drive, Suite 200
Bloomington, IN 47403
www.authorhouse.com
Phone: 1-800-839-8640

First published by AuthorHouse 2/28/2008

ISBN: 978-1-4343-6016-8 (sc)

Library of Congress Control Number: 2007910377

The publisher and the author disclaim liablilty for any outcomes that may occur as a result from applying the methods as suggested in this book.

Printed in the United States of America
Bloomington, Indiana

This book is printed on acid-free paper.

This book is dedicated to the 47 million people in America* who are uninsured, the working class, who are the heart and soul of our country. These are factory, industry, service and hourly retail workers who are the backbone of this nation. They are hard working individuals with families, hopes and dreams. However, so many of our working poor lack the proper health care so desperately needed and deserved. I hope this book will help change the way our country views the importance of adequate health care coverage for everyone. It is not a privilege; it is something that should be accessible to all Americans.

Anne Boston Parish

---

*   John Donnelly, "47 million Americans are uninsured," The Boston Globe, August 29, 2007. http://www.boston.com/news/washington/articles/2007/29/47_million_americans...

To laugh often and much
To win the respect of intelligent people and the
affection of children; to earn the appreciation
Of honest critics and
Endure the betrayal of false friends;
To appreciate beauty
To find the best in others;
to leave the world a bit better, whether by a
healthy child, a garden patch, or a redeemed
social condition.
To know even one life has breathed easier
Because you have lived.
This is to have succeeded.

- Ralph Waldo Emerson

CONTENTS

ACKNOWLEDGMENTS

I want to thank my beloved parents, Ward and Emma Boston, who have always unconditionally supported me in whatever direction my life has taken; my student, Ms. Alana Rae Noritake, a summer intern from the College of William and Mary who transferred seven years of writing from floppy discs to CD-ROMs and helped develop the content and details. Completing this book would not have been possible without Mr. John Riddle, author and freelance writer who edited the manuscript, the Nurse Practitioner and Physician Assistant students for whom I have served as preceptor; and to my loyal patients who call Queen Street Clinic their medical home. I am grateful that these patients believed in me and allowed me to provide them medical care and most of all, to tell their stories. This has been an abundantly generous gift.

I also want to acknowledge Chris Ford and Taylor Burke at Burke & Herbert Bank & Trust in Alexandria. They believed enough in my dream to extend to me a mortgage to purchase the building to house the clinic. Much appreciation goes to the Navy Federal Credit Union, which provided the funds for the build-out. I am grateful to the entire team of contractors and my carpenter, Michael Farrell of

Farrell Construction, with whom the clinic doors would not have opened. I am indebted to the former Mayor of Alexandria, Kerry Donley, who wrote a beautifully drafted letter that facilitated the in-kind donations from those who helped with the build-out. Additionally, a thanks goes to Ken Fanelli, who offered his editing assistance and believed in this project from the beginning. To the entire team of *authorHouse*, your efforts did not go unnoticed.

In particular, I would like to mention my dear children, Jennifer Parish Wallace and George Rod Parish IV, who challenged me to follow this dream. I am blessed to have brought them into this world and to be their mother. The newest additions to my family are George and Gracie, my English Bull Dogs. Their companionship, their unconditional love, and lively spirits were an invaluable comfort through the entire process of writing this book.

All of this would not have been possible without the encouragement of my many mentors who were instrumental in my professional development. Their friendship and continual encouragement to build the clinic motivated me to persevere, despite all the challenges inherent in such a process. I also want to express my deep gratitude to my family and colleagues, both named and unnamed, in this book for their constant cheer.

Last, I would like to extend my deepest appreciation to the present mayor of Alexandria, William Euille, whose influence was instrumental in the formation of the clinic. His long-term friendship, support and endorsement for my efforts at the clinic continue to be appreciated.

City of Alexandria, Virginia
301 King Street, Suite 2300
Alexandria, Virginia 22314

William D. Euille
Mayor

City Hall (703) 838-4500
Home (703) 836-2680
Fax (703) 838-6433
alexvamayor@aol.com

"Anne Parish"

Like Mother Teresa, Anne Parish felt a calling early in life to be a service to mankind, first as a nurse, and now as a medical practitioner serving the poor.

Like Mother Teresa, Anne Parish, believes "it is not how much we do, but how much love we put in the doing. It is not how much we give, but how much love we put in the giving".

Anne is indeed a Saint, in the eyes of those to whom she has served in ensuring that they receive medical attention and care in order to live a fruitful and happy life. This is her mission...this is her life.

As a life long resident of Alexandria, where we cherish our diversity-social, economic and racial, we have many challenges, and government relies on our local businesses, faith based, non-profits and others to help our citizens in need. Anne and her Queen Street Clinic has answered the call by treating approximately 20,000 patient visits since opening in 2001, in helping to promote a healthier Alexandria.

I am honored to have met Anne, share in her vision, and now watch how she has blossomed like a flower and spread her petals with love, affection and hope for Alexandria's less fortunate.

Ann is a "Living Legend" in Alexandria.

Anne, Godspeed.

Always,

William D. Euille
Mayor

"Home Town of George Washington and Robert E. Lee"

Letter from the Mayor

VISION AND THINKING OUTSIDE OF THE BOX

This is a book about vision and the reality of the delivery of the American health care system. It is about challenges and hurdles. It is a book that searches for answers. It is a book that looks into the future and asks the question not why, but why not? Some people are blessed with the ability to see the future. I was fortunate enough to see a glimpse of the future and the evolution of health care for those without health care insurance. Anyone who is able to think outside of the box should read this book, which may be of value to those who have vision and can share my philosophy. The prospect of working long hours and learning to wear different hats should not dissuade you from living a dream: establishing a community clinic of your own. I searched for literature to use as a tool for designing a clinic on a limited budget and could not find a suitable book. So, from personal experience comes this book. Remember, nothing of value ever comes easy.

Eight years ago, I noticed there was a need to provide health care to the medically uninsured. At that time I had been working in a skilled nursing facility providing health care to those who had already been assigned a bed, knowing that would be their last home. One evening, as I wandered the halls of the facility, I wondered why the patients who were not yet elderly were suffering from debilitating illnesses. Most of these patients were in their early 50s, yet were approaching the end of their lives with little hope of leaving that facility. Many were missing limbs, were hooked up to oxygen, or were in renal failure. Most of these conditions were the results of untreated diabetes, emphysema, heart disease, ovarian cancer, breast cancer, or hypertension — all of which are easily managed if caught in the early stages. These patients' medical needs had been left unattended. These patients were now in the final stages of the diseases and awaiting death…how tragic! My initial thought was, *Why have their illnesses been allowed to progress to the advanced stage of chronic disease?* The answer was simple; these patients had been denied the benefits of preventative medicine. They were unable to afford health care insurance, or had never been offered it. As a result, their health care had been neglected until their conditions were chronic and their prognoses and medical outcomes were very poor. I knew at that moment I needed to do something to help the medically uninsured. Over the last seven years, I have observed a growing population of patients who choose not to purchase health care plans, even though afforded the opportunity to buy into a medical policy, through their employer. I am not referring to these patients; I am referring to those patients in the skilled facility knowing this was their last home.

For many without health care insurance their only option is the hospital emergency room. In many cases, these working poor fall into a group that is not privileged enough to buy health care plans. Employers may not have offered them a health care option, or if one is offered they may be unable to afford the cost. Has health insurance become a luxury? I think that in some cases it has. Unfortunately, many of these families fall between the cracks. They do not qualify for eligibility because their income is too high to qualify for public health assistance. Our health care system is not able to meet the needs of the working poor, both young and old.

One day, shortly after I had participated in a teleconference with VHA, a hospital organization in Irving, Texas, I received the following letter from Dr. John J. Collins, Jr. I was flattered and surprised that Dr. Collins would take the time to write such a thoughtful letter, especially since writing letters appears to have gone out of style. He had hand written a letter to me, and I was impressed. When I read his words, I not only felt very much appreciated, it made my mission that much more important. I was determined — more than ever — to continue my journey and to help those who are less fortunate. I wanted to work even harder to provide health care in my community. I had made an impression on a physician outside of my community, who was inspired by my efforts. What a nice compliment! And from this, I will begin my story.

December 7, 2001

Dear Anne,

Thank you for spending the hour with our team this morning. Your passion-commitment-advocacy-perseverance-and expertise is very apparent and contagious! I found myself longing to be back on the front lines of health care serving people in need.

As we work to find hospital members willing to take on a project for the uninsured in their communities the vision and reality of what you are doing sets the quality standard.

Congratulations, thanks and best wishes.

John

[sic]

My mission was to design a practical solution for those without health insurance. My philosophy was simple: if you keep people healthy, it will prevent the long-term ill effects of chronic illness (prevention, prevention, prevention!). Many individuals who do not have health insurance seek care only after the medical condition has degenerated into a chronic, debilitating illness. For these individuals, the fear of lost wages and savings and the fear of death become overwhelming. For others who are unable to continue employment, their greatest fear becomes a reality. They become burdens to society and their families. The loss of their jobs, their homes, and their worldly possessions — for which they have worked a lifetime — breaks their spirits. They become resentful, bitter, and angry with a system that has failed them. Has the system failed them, or had they not prepared themselves for an unforeseen medical malady that forces them to enter social programs? For some it was not having access to health insurance, for others, it is not having enrolled into medical insurance plans.

As a result, many of our social programs have become overwhelmed and financially drained. The sheer number of these individuals requiring immediate attention following diagnoses of chronic diseases creates a backup of appointments in regular clinics. At some clinics, there are two-month waiting periods to be seen. Most of these patients cannot wait that long and are forced to make multiple trips to the hospital emergency room. In turn, this floods the emergency rooms with non-emergent cases and inhibits the emergency room staff in its ability to handle life-threatening medical emergencies. Using the emergency room for non-emergent care is inappropriate, especially when these cases could be treated in a family practice facility in a timely fashion, at a fraction of the cost.

When I opened the clinic, the greatest obstacle I had to overcome was to market the concept of competent, affordable and accessible health care. Initially, many patients assumed the clinic was free, particularly since they had no experience outside of government-funded care. Many would have thought *no one person* could have designed and built a medical model to support the working poor. I built the clinic from my own personal funds, and have worked hard to maintain the operational status from the first day. Queen Street Clinic has made a huge impact on the wellness of Alexandria and its surrounding community. Prior to its opening, there was not a clinic to support the medical needs for those groups who were medically uninsured.

My patient population is not unique. Across the United States are countless communities that do not have community clinics that provide access to health care for this population that I call the working poor. As mentioned previously, I saw in the skilled nursing facilities numerous patients who could have been living normal and fulfilling lives had their medical conditions simply been addressed earlier.

Nothing is so powerful as
"An idea whose time has come."

– Victor Hugo

PART I

MISCONCEPTIONS ABOUT THIS TYPE OF CLINIC: DISPELLING THE MYTH

Health Care Leadership and Misconceptions about Clinics

Health care reform is a topic many want to address. However, few have implemented viable solutions for the growing epidemic of the medically uninsured. Being without health insurance instills fear in many people. It has become a personal assault that an ever-increasing number of Americans face, which forces them to choose between paying for medical care and buying food to feed their families. For many, an acute or chronic medical crisis finds them without a medical home for care. There are many Americans who have experienced the uncertainty of not knowing where to turn if a serious illness occurs, or if routine health care is needed, fear the "what ifs?" If I become ill, where will I receive care? Many of these feelings are experienced on a daily basis as individuals feel the despair of watching a family member or friend have no option but to turn to the hospital emergency room. Too many people, having forfeited nearly everything in the pursuit of health care, have lost all hope of leading normal lives. They are constantly in fear of the bill collector or of having wages garnished.

I am reminded of the inspirational Biblical phrase: "For those who have been given much, much is expected" [*Luke 12:48*]. When I opened the clinic, I knew the journey would be difficult. I knew there would be challenges; however, I never expected that in such an affluent community, with so many of privilege, there would be so little support for my small part of the solution to the growing problem of those without health care. For many of my patients, the clinic was the beginning of hope and an answer to the exorbitant cost of health care. I knew my cause was larger than myself. I was not willing to ignore what I know is a sensible solution to a growing epidemic — those in my community without health insurance. I just needed a forum to awaken the consciousness of the community.

A few years ago, I wrote an article for a local newspaper in the hopes of stimulating awareness of the growing epidemic of those without health insurance. The purpose of the article was to awaken the spirit of those who have health insurance with the intent that those who have been given much would give to those less fortunate. I was discouraged by the lack of response from readers who had the wherewithal to support the efforts of the clinic. At that time, I had far exceeded my own personal challenge and surprised many in the community as the clinic entered its fourth year of operation. My patient numbers clearly demonstrated a need for the clinic, and the high percentage of patients who considered the clinic their medical home was greater than even I had imagined. I developed one workable solution to our growing epidemic of the medically uninsured. However, it requires more than one article or one person to awaken the altruistic spirit and conscience of the community and to make its residents see what seems so clear to me.

The clinic is a small business and, as such, I am not privileged to receive grant money or city, state, or federal funds. I built the clinic out of my private funds, and I continue to offer health care for the working poor. I am not unique solely because I provide care for those less fortunate. Many medical practitioners do this. I believe I am different because I am a sole provider who chooses not to work with insurance companies as a means to keep the cost of an office visit to a minimum. I have developed partnerships with outside agencies to offer laboratory and imaging at discounted rates. In essence, these discounted prices allow patients to receive ordered laboratory and imaging within their budgets. (See Appendix: Queen Street Clinic Price Menu.)

The clinic also serves as a champion for many patients who might not be able to afford their medications by enrolling them in patient assistance programs with various pharmaceutical companies. I am also very fortunate to develop working relationships with many specialty physicians who support my family practice efforts and to whom I can refer my patients for specialty care. The last piece of the puzzle that makes the whole concept of the clinic's mission possible is the assistance I receive from local churches, which frequently, on an individual basis, assists patients who need medical care but cannot afford it.

I have learned that the concept of the word "clinic" denotes the idea that it is *free*. When I think about the clinic, I think of openness, fairness, equitable care, and — of course — medical care at a reasonable cost. The care that is provided is safe, excellent, and prudent in its delivery. Frequently, I have spent much of my day, as well as the clinic staffs' time, trying to educate my patient population and the community that the concept of "clinic" does not connote it is "free" care.

Oftentimes, patients do not understand that the care I provide is not without cost. The daily operational costs that include the "silent" or indirect costs are costs that most people do not think about unless they are directly involved in paying incoming invoices. If you do not operate a small business, you normally do not think about the additional costs that are incurred in the daily operation of the business. This overhead is usually not included in the fee for service for an office visit. The revenue needed to absorb the indirect costs comes from working long hours and never turning away a potential patient.

While the clinic is functioning, additional charges a patient may incur are added to the office visit fee, and may include laboratory work (e.g., complete blood count [CBC]) or possibly a procedure performed in the office. This might include a urinalysis, rapid throat culture, or a pregnancy test. These tests are purchased by the clinic, and the costs to perform them are not something that can be included in the office visit fee. It is an operational expense. Durable medical supplies need to be purchased in order to perform these office procedures, and the charges are nominal for the testing provided.

The imaging component, if one is needed for a diagnosis, is directly paid to the imaging center (e.g., Examination of Electromagnetic Radiation [X-ray], Magnetic Resonance Imaging [MRI] or Computerized Tomography [CT]) and is an additional charge for the patient even though it is deeply discounted.

Every day more Americans face the crisis of health care coverage. Your clinic will offer competent, affordable and accessible health care. It will become the medical home for those people, in the community, who are without medical health insurance. Recently I heard on a radio talk show that the percentage of people who earn less than $20,000 per year is 36 percent of the working population. Those who earn less than $25,000 per year rank at 33 percent without health insurance; and only three percent of those who earn at or greater than $50,000 per year are without health insurance. Those individuals or families who rank in that staggering figure between 33 and 36 percent — and who are without health insurance — will become your primary patient population.

"The purpose of life is a life with purpose."

- Robert Byrne

PART II

DARE TO TAKE THE CHALLENGE

I have designed one solution to this growing epidemic of the medically uninsured. The purpose of this book is to provide health care advocates, educators, investors and communities across the United States access to a successful medical model in the delivery of health care for the medically uninsured. There will be others who will read this book, because he or she has an interest in their community's well being, and he or she want to educate their community leaders about the growing epidemic of the medically uninsured.

When I first opened the clinic, the estimated number of medically uninsured residents in Alexandria, Virginia was approaching 25 percent; today the number continues to escalate and is estimated at 29 percent. This same trend of increased numbers of uninsured Americans is being seen in cities outside of Alexandria. According to a report issued by the Centers for

Disease Control and Prevention, "In 2005, more then 40 million adults did not receive 'needed services' because they could not afford them."*

I met the challenge, and I believe more uninsured and under-insured Americans would benefit by availing themselves to this convenient and effective model of health care. There is no reason other communities should not replicate this model and give health care to patients who desperately need the option of a competent, affordable medical home. Rising costs of emergency room care are indirectly raising taxes that could be better utilized for other social programs. If a single-provider clinic can make such an impact without benefit of state, federal, and city funds, imagine what could be accomplished with community-wide support for this model of care. I believe it would provide an important part of the solution to the growing epidemic of our medically uninsured.

---

* Maggie Fox, "Over 40 million in U.S. can't afford health care: report," REUTERS, December 3, 2007. http://www.reuters.com/articleId=USN0343703420071203. See "www.cdc.gov/nchs/"

Learn to Believe in More Than You Can See

If you think you are someone who can make things happen, then establishing a clinic may be the new adventure for which you've been looking. I believe life is a journey and not a destination. I am still on that journey, and on a daily basis I am reminded by my patients that my journey is still ongoing. Some days are more difficult than others; however, at the end of the day, I am always able to find the good that comes out of providing health care to those who are less fortunate. I was able to visualize a clinic that offered a haven for those without a medical home. In the beginning of my journey, the days were long and I struggled with overcoming many hurdles. The faith I had in myself brought the miracle of the Queen Street Clinic to life

Keep Your Eye on the Prize!

The most frequently posed question is how an idea became a functioning clinic. In response, I have written an outline from the planning stages of the Queen Street Clinic up to the operational phase. The heart of the book lies within the pages of my writing and the passion I felt as I pursued my dream. If building a clinic is something you want to do, I encourage you to embrace that purpose in your life. Dreams are almost always bigger than you are. This means you must reach to make them come true.

Outline your time frame, project, personal and professional goals as a small business owner and clinician. As you undertake this, you may hear that inner voice cheering you on. Only then will you find the place where you will discover inner peace and professional growth. Rather than reinvent the wheel, use this book to assess your skills and your community resources. Keep your eye on the prize, and don't lose sight of the goal in the journey you are about to begin.

Let my journey be a learning experience when pursuing your dream. Use this book to assess your motivation and determination to build a clinic. My knowledge, perspective and experience will steer you through and over the obstacles I learned to hurdle. I kept my eye on the prize! Prizes come in every shape, form and size. Your prize will be a clinic that offers your community a safe haven for providing health care. The rewards are endless and priceless.

Evaluate your community and look beyond what you can see; for it is faith that brings miracles to light.

Sole Proprietor

Once you have established you are going to build and own a clinic, be mindful that anything valuable and successful requires long hours, time, energy and money — and it will own you. You may be lucky and have a colleague who shares your vision and is willing to devote his or her efforts in the start-up and the ownership of a successful clinic. For my business, I remain the sole proprietor, and all of the responsibility of the clinic belongs to me. If I have only one suggestion to offer, it is to find a partner who would share some of the physical and financial responsibility. If you don't bring in a partner — especially as the business grows — you will have a difficult time letting go of the full ownership because of the emotional tie. At times, in the early stages of building the clinic, the financial investment and the "sweat equity" will overwhelm you. On occasion, I needed to explain that the operation of such a business is not without personal sacrifice, and I frequently would tell patients, "I mortgaged my home to build the clinic." Although, throughout the process of building the clinic, I never doubted, and knew my efforts would succeed. I always knew that if I could open the doors, the clinic would be fully operational.

The clinic remains true to its original mission and structure: continuing to provide health care at an affordable price without the use of state, local, or federal funding. Unlike funded public health clinics or medical practices that receive grant monies or take medical insurance for patient care, the clinic operates solely from revenue generated by patient care. Frequently patients erroneously assume that the City of Alexandria subsidizes the clinic or that the clinic has a 501(c) 3 nonprofit status.

As the clinic's founder, owner, and sole proprietor I have found that unless you understand the depth and breadth of a Nurse Practitioner education, you may find many questioning how you are able to provide health care because you are not a physician. In the early years of operation, this seemed to be a great concern. Although, as the clinic's good reputation circulated, very few people were concerned being treated by a Nurse Practitioner. I now find very few people questioning my title as Nurse Practitioner. I am exceedingly proud of being a Nurse Practitioner. Likewise, I am pleased to say I built the clinic, and am its founder and owner. In the United States, each state varies with the privilege of independent practice for the Nurse Practitioner. It is important to research your state for practice guidelines and how your scope of practice and the guidelines are in compliance with the Board of Medicine and Nursing.

A Multi-Tier System

When I think of the word "multi-tier" I think of levels that progress upward to a platform. In theory, the platform symbolizes a realistic solution for America's broken health care delivery system. I saw the platform as one solution for the delivery of affordable and accessible medical care. The platform was the medical model that I had designed — the Queen Street Clinic. Before you can describe a solution you need to define the problem. So, I defined the problem. Our present day medical model is failing so many and meeting the needs of too few. I saw the lack of America's health care delivery system defined as being multi-tier in structure or hierarchy.

Over the last seven years, I have witnessed individuals go in and out of insurance plans, individuals decline insurance options, and families struggle after a catastrophic event. I have witnessed individuals denied health care coverage because of pre-existing conditions and I have seen individuals not privileged to afford health care medical plans. The media tends to focus on high-profile cancer patients who have the means to seek the best treatment coupled with the most qualified medical providers for their care. What happens to those who need the same level of care but who are not as privileged? What does this say about our society? What is the future for those who are without health care coverage? Who will take care of them? I do not believe Uncle Sam needs to be the single payer for the nation's health care bills, but there needs to be a balance in the delivery of health care that is competent, accessible, and affordable. No one should be denied access for health care because he or she can not pay.

Nowhere in my community was there a clinic that was built solely for the needs of those who are medically uninsured. Within my market analysis I had identified five reasons for being medically uninsured. Over the last seven years I have provided health care for individuals who could be categorized, in one or in all of the five reasons, for being medically uninsured. Now, more than ever, I am confident and sure, that I am filling a large void in my community for individuals who are in need of a medical home. The following five examples illustrate the multi-tier system that exists across America:

+ Those who utilized the public health services (indigent population) and pay out of pocket for an acute or chronic medical condition
+ Those who are not offered health insurance, by their employer, and pay out of pocket for an acute or chronic medical condition
+ Those who are offered health care insurance, by their employer, but who choose not to purchase a plan, and pay out of pocket for an acute or chronic medical condition
+ Those who have pre-existing conditions, and are denied health care coverage, and pay out of pocket for their pre-existing condition.

+ Those who are priced out of affordable health insurance and pay out of pocket for an acute or chronic medical condition

I am equally as confident that there are many medically insured individuals who are willing to pay out of pocket to be seen at the Queen Street Clinic. I have listed a few reasons why an individual, with medical insurance, would pay for an acute or chronic condition.

+ Convenience
+ Not being able to be seen by his or her primary care provider in a timely fashion for an acute or chronic condition
+ He or she appreciates the patient care that is extended by the clinic
+ The clinic is accessible and affordable
+ He or she trusts the care that is prudent, safe and competent

Imagine a large repository or "warehouse" of names and lists of individuals who have already been labeled "medically uninsured." In this warehouse these individuals move from one tier to another only hoping that one day they will be privileged to purchase medical coverage. America's health care system is broken and I wanted to design a viable solution to the problem. To acknowledge there is a problem is the easy part. The difficult task is to educate and motivate those in my community that the Queen Street Clinic was a viable solution. In my effort to define the problem, I had to educate the public that the clinic would be an option for the medically uninsured. I asked myself again, did I want to take this challenge? You know the answer by now, it was yes.

One of the important reasons for starting a business is for your satisfaction and self-actualization. My goal is to make the world a better place. After opening the clinic doors, I had to educate and communicate this concept to many patients reminding them that nowhere in my office policies is it stated my clinic is a "free clinic." Many new patients could not believe and were shocked to learn the clinic was built without local, state or federal funding. In essence, one of the most difficult concepts to convey to this patient population is he or she is taking charge of his or her health care and he or she is responsible for payment. The collection of payment in a fee-for-service clinic can be one of the most difficult challenges you will ever have to overcome. The idea that one is entitled to health care is not unreasonable; however, many individuals believe that the American public health service model should apply to all clinics across the board, regardless of how the health care facility is built.

When a person tells me he or she cannot pay for care, I remind myself that our society has never educated the public about the costs in the delivery of health care. Most individuals who lack health insurance do not understand the indirect operational costs involved in the maintenance of a health clinic. A few examples include: licensing fees, professional dues, and — of course — just paying the utilities that provide heating, cooling, and electricity. For those who fall in the category of indigent care, medical examinations and treatment are provided at no charge or on a sliding scale. Much of that care is determined through an eligibility process, and the patients receive their care through the public health department. In 2006, according to U.S. Census Bureau data, the United States had over 47 million medically uninsured individuals. This is largely due to cutbacks in employer-sponsored health coverage. Of these, according to a federal government report released in December 2007, 40 million people in this country claim they cannot afford adequate health care and forego drugs, eyeglasses and dental treatment. This is despite the fact that the United States spends more on health care per capita than any other nation.

Increasingly, health care coverage is no longer offered in a company's employee benefits package. Many companies are beginning to reserve the right to deny individuals health care policies as a result of pre-existing medical conditions. Where do these individuals go if they are forced into early retirement or buy-outs? The cruel irony is that many deserving individuals may never be reinstated in new health plans if they possess a pre-existing medical condition. There is also a large population of individuals who either cannot afford their employer's health care plan that is offered or are not offered the plan because of part time work falls below the required minimum to earn that benefit. I soon learned that there is also a growing population of individuals who are offered health care insurance, but declined purchasing a plan. Last, there are those who are in between jobs and cannot afford the hefty Consolidated Omnibus Budget Reconciliation Act [COBRA] payments necessary to continue health coverage. Consequently, in the event of a health care crisis, many deserving people are left without the security of a medical home. The reality for those individuals who can purchase a plan, but declined enrollment in a medical policy, are gambling that they will never experience a medical illness or unforeseen catastrophic event.

Once I had a patient who was an American missionary nun in Kenya. She said, "The Africans believe [that] if you do not believe in yourself and trust your decision-making skills, how can they believe and trust in you?" So, always remember, *"Believe in more than you can see, for it is faith that brings miracles to life!"* (*Source unknown*) Your presence in the community sends a powerful message: Health care is not a privilege. It should be competent, accessible and affordable. Health care should be available for all Americans regardless of race, ethnic or cultural background, economic status or religion.

Learn to trust yourself, your leadership style and your ability to make accurate decisions. Do not yield to the pressures you may feel to compromise your standards and the clinic's mission. The clinic, along with your ability to build, operate, and provide health care is priceless. For many patients, you will make a diagnosis that will save their lives. For other patients with chronic diseases, you will lessen their fears. For many patients, you will treat an acute illness that has been poorly managed. Remember, your knowledge of medicine, health care and your ability to operate your clinic is vital, and you must remind yourself how much your community is counting on you for the services you provide.

Personal Reflections on Starting a Business

Some Reasons People Start Businesses:

+ To become rich and famous
+ Self actualization
+ To help others—altruism
+ Personal challenge
+ Enjoyment in the field of work
+ To be a business owner
+ To make the world and the community a better place
+ To offer a service that no one else offers
+ Ability to take business write-offs
+ Are risk takers

Challenges You Never Thought You Would Experience:

+ Long hours
+ Debt
+ Bills
+ High utilities
+ Malpractice insurance
+ Commercial insurance
+ Taxes
+ Cleaning the bathroom and waiting area after working a long day
+ Maintenance of the property
+ Staffing problems
+ The need to open on schedule regardless of the weather

+ Feeling unappreciated
+ Negative Feedback

Decisions You Will Want To Make:

+ Do I buy or rent a location for the clinic?
+ Do I rebuild and renovate a run-down empty building?
+ If I buy, can I secure a loan?
+ Do I mortgage my home to secure a loan to buy a run-down property?
+ Will I be able to secure enough money with "in-kind donations" to rebuild a building in disrepair?
+ Will the seller show up for closing? If he or she does not go to settlement, do I retain an attorney and file a lawsuit for "breach of specific performance"?
+ Can I afford to retain a good attorney who will quickly win the case and not prolong the litigation?
+ Am I prepared to pay for every minute spent speaking to an attorney?

I have listed phrases for you to use in an inventory of your leadership strengths and weaknesses. Do not consider a weakness a failure, but a means of identifying inner growth. Reflecting on your weaknesses and practicing to overcome them is a learned behavior. Before you take on the role as the owner of a small business, review these phrases and make an effort to define your personality style.

+ Communicating a vision
+ Ability to see outside of the box
+ Implementing a goal

- Valuation of service that you will provide
- Philosophy of business and self
- Ability to establish rules
- Changing new ideas about the delivery of health care
- Support of family, partner and friends
- Discipline and time management
- Balancing both personal and professional life
- Autonomy of self
- Professional satisfaction
- Self-confidence
- Ability to manage conflict
- Communicating problems
- Handling stress
- Outlet for stress
- Motivating staff
- Managing staff and their accountability
- Understanding commitment from your staff or partners
- Overcoming bad attitude and vindictive behavior
- Self-respect
- Knowledge of your cash flow and your assets
- Risk taking
- Fear of failure
- Role of power
- Expressing results that have been achieved
- Ability to set limits for yourself and others
- Ability to motivate others who have your vision
- Nurturing staff
- Ability to terminate staff

- Ability to engage staff in daily tasks and ownership of their duties
- Nurturing students
- Marketing an idea or concept
- Understanding your leadership style
- Being an active listener
- Implementing new skills or techniques
- Having empathy
- Ability to communicate test results and provide comfort
- Being able to provide reassurance
- Trust in colleagues
- Community acceptance and support
- Professional networking and acceptance
- Understanding diverse cultural perspectives
- Spirituality and expectations with health and illness
- Being able to handle rejection, criticism and sometimes cruel words
- Being true to yourself and those around you
- Learning to be good to yourself
- The business you own, can own you too
- The difficulties inherent in taking time off
- Reflecting daily on the reasons why you built the clinic
- Consequences and aftermath of failure

NOTE: This list is not intended to identify personality types but is useful in self-reflection.

Yesterday is history,
Tomorrow is mystery,
Today is a gift.

- Eleanor Roosevelt

PART III

BUILDING BLOCKS: HOW TO LAUNCH A CLINIC

The Idea:

- Marketing the concept of an affordable health care option
- Fee for service
- No governmental funds
- No eligibility requirements
- Discounted laboratory fees and discounted imaging fees
- Enrolling patients in pharmaceutical patient assistance drug programs
- Specialty physicians for referrals
- Free mammograms for eligible Alexandria residents
- Free trial samples of medications

Ownership

- ✦ A business partner
- ✦ Shared responsibility
- ✦ Flexibility
- ✦ Taking time off
- ✦ Maintaining a sense of balance
- ✦ Revenue

I strongly encourage you to find a business partner. A partner is support for the daily responsibilities of the running of a clinic. While this may include the patient care, more importantly, it provides both partners flexibility and freedom to take vacations. Taking time off is necessary for maintaining your mental health and is ideal for pursuing professional growth (e.g., to attend continuing education classes, workshops, etc.). It is important to not allow your business to own you. Ownership is demanding and requires more than working an eight-hour day. Oftentimes in ownership, you do not have the freedom to pursue outside interests, due to the demands of being responsible for the multitude of tasks required of the self-employed. Even after seven years, I still do not have a steady flow of income. I take an owner's draw when I need to address my financial demands. For many who are self-employed, being paid on a regular basis is not a guarantee. If you are the type of person who needs to be gainfully employed and paid on a weekly or bi-weekly basis, perhaps owning a business is not for you. Cash flow usually improves when a second medical provider joins the staff. The revenue generated by this position often allows both partners to be paid salaries.

Mission Statement

+ Focus
+ Goals
+ Purpose
+ Clarification
+ Funding

One of the first tasks I completed was to write a mission statement that focuses on the delivery of health care. This has been an invaluable tool to define the clinic's goals and purpose and offers a framework for the clinic's rules and policies. It hangs prominently in the lobby of the clinic and describes my purpose. The mission statement also defines the clinic as a small business defining that it is not privileged to receive state, local, federal or not-for-profit money. It operates solely by the fees charged for an office visit.

I truly believe every business should develop a mission statement and display it in the lobby. This clearly defines who you are, your motivation to provide the service, and the expectation that is offered by the business. A clinic needs to clearly state its intentions as a not-for profit entity or a small business. This can resolve any confusion relating to eligibility for local, state, or federal funding. On more than one occasion, I have had to show the mission statement to patients that do not understand that the clinic was built with my own funds.

The Confidentiality Policy, State Reportable Disease List, Health Insurance Portability, Privacy Rule, Accountability, and Public Health Act of 1996 (HIPPA) should be displayed in the public area. I would strongly recommend that the Clinic Rules be prominently displayed.

Location, Location, Location

+ Find the right location
+ Secure a location walking distance from the bus and rail lines
+ Locate your office in the central business district of town

Finding the right location is truly one of the most important tasks you will accomplish. When I began my search for a building to house the clinic, my first priority was to find a building walking distance of bus and light rail lines. A clinic needs to be located in the central business district of town. This enables the patients who lack transportation the ability to travel to and from referred services (specialty physicians, laboratories and imaging centers).

Securing the Site for the Clinic

- Do you want to purchase or lease a space?
- Is the space habitable?
- Will there be renovation expenses?
- Can you find contractors (i.e., electricians, heating and air-conditioning specialists, plumbers, masons and carpenters) to assist in the renovation?
- Should you be your own general contractor?
- Can you finding a carpenter?
- Do you know how to research the building's chain of title for any defects or existing liens (i.e., tax liens, mechanics' liens or court judgments) on the property?
- Do you have the available time to visits city government offices for permits, plans and zoning approvals?

Securing a site for the clinic was the first task I needed to complete. I wanted to purchase a building. For me this was a personal choice. Leasing is also an option. Once I found the building, I knew I needed to make the necessary renovations. That requires considerable capital. I decided purchasing the building would be a better investment because I now have better control over future associated costs. I found a building in need of repair. I knew that with a fresh coat of paint, a fair amount of elbow grease and some minor building renovation it could become a clinic.

Finding contractors to support me in the renovation was the next task. I approached various contractors in the community who proved to be very generous during the remodeling process. These contractors included an electrician, heating and air conditioning contractor, a plumber and a good carpenter.

I became the general contractor, because the job was considered too small for a typical construction overseer to handle. I developed a plan of action, outlining the steps I needed to implement for securing building permits, and other city documents necessary for the city inspector's sign-off.

When I made the decision to become the general contractor, I signed a city affidavit that I would be ultimately responsible for the work being done to the building. I had hired a carpenter to assist me with the heavier construction. The various contractors who agreed to assist were responsible for securing their own specialty permits, and the work was subject to city inspections prior to the issuance of a Certificate of Occupancy.

Prior to purchasing the structure, I researched the building itself. Any property must be zoned for commercial purposes. (See Appendix: letter from the City of Alexandria's Department of Planning and Zoning.) Ensure your efforts are not wasted on an unsuitable site for a future clinic.

Planning is critical in the beginning phase of establishing a medical clinic. To succeed, refer to this outline. Review the following checklist for the steps necessary in the renovation of a building you will occupy as your prospective clinic. Requirements may vary from city to city or state to state.

- Blueprints from an architect are needed to secure permits to ensure that the space is adequate for its use and to provide detail for any enclosures.

- Permits from the Code Enforcement Office and from the Department of Planning and Zoning.

- An application to appear before the Board of Architectural Review (BAR). This building was in a historic district, so the historic character of the build-out needed to be preserved. This included permission to hang a clinic sign as well as compliance with standards for sign size and overall appearance.

- Blueprints were needed to conform to guidelines of the American Disability Act (ADA) inspection for adequately sized doors and a bathroom for the disabled. In some jurisdictions, existing facilities are "grandfathered" depending on the extent of construction. While this may save considerable cost, one has to consider the negative impact this may have on the patient population; because the bathroom may not adequately allow someone in a wheelchair to access the facilities.

- A Certificate of Occupancy. This is the last document needed to complete the renovation of the building. At this point, all specific permits were signed off, and the final inspection had been done.

Never, never, never give up!

— Winston Churchill

PART IV

THE BUSINESS PLAN

To build a clinic, a business plan is a good formula for success. Many businesses use figures within an allotted budget. I began reviewing capital expenses such as an electrocardiogram (e.g., an EKG or ECG machine). I spoke to a few banks that provided me with some idea of the costs that would be incurred in securing a loan to purchase the building. In 2000, I found startup costs for opening the clinic to be in the range of $100,000 to $200,000. This did not include the purchase of the building.

My first appointment was with the mayor of Alexandria to discuss my project. He provided me with a wonderful letter to support the building of the clinic. This letter offered important substantial support (See Letter from the Mayor).

The second stop was to solicit the attention and support from the contractors who would be making the necessary structural changes to the building. I was very fortunate because much of the cost that I incurred was provided at a discounted rate. The rest was donated. As I approached the different contractors, I showed each a copy of the letter from the mayor. This one letter was extraordinarily instrumental in their decision to back my efforts during construction. This endorsement was like gold in my hands because it validated its purpose. As a result, I was able to secure over $41,000 dollars of in-kind donations to for the build-out.

After I obtained the approval of the contractors, I needed to secure a loan. To buy the building, I first had to take a second mortgage on my own home. Initially, this was a difficult decision. I had no other business partner who could help defray the start-up costs. So, without hesitation, I mortgaged my home. A quote I held dear by Mary Lyon: *Trust in God and do something.*

After deciding what type of arrangement you wish to pursue — whether purchasing a building or leasing an office space — be mindful there are up-front costs to begin. When you to develop your business plan, you must identify a dollar amount for projected capital expenses (anything exceeding $500).

Below is a template for projected start-up costs. Forecast a dollar figure to support the necessary expenses for the projected year and a cost analysis of your financial outcome along with a break-even analysis. Depending on where you locate your business, the fees and costs will vary. There may be supplemental requirements depending on the county, city, or state.

Projected Costs and Capital for
Start-Up of the Clinic

BANK/LEASING A SITE	Anticipated capital
Loan or monthly fee	
Capital for build-out and labor	
Equity loan on personal assets	

BUILDOUT AND LABOR	Project the cost per line item
New Roof	
HVAC (Heat and Air)	
Gas Line	
Electrical	
Demo of building/hauling trash	
Building material for construction	
Plumbing (bathroom/water heater)	
Security System	
Paint	
Outside clinic signs	
Flooring	
Carpenter fee	
Architectural fee for blueprints	

BANK ACCOUNTS	$100.00 minimum per account
Operational	
Merchant	
Payroll	
Tax	

It is important to establish multiple bank accounts to keep funds separate and safeguard the business financially. It is essential to reconcile your financial books monthly and quarterly. It is important to ensure the correct deposits are put in the appropriate account and that operational funds reflect money collected by the clinic. Secure bank accounts as soon as possible. Until the clinic was opened, I wrote checks from my personal checking account and kept accurate records of payment. Afterwards, you may pay yourself back for your initial start-up costs; of course this may take time.

PROFESSIONAL FEES	Fees vary
State Board (RN/FNP/ Authorize to Prescribe)	
DEA (Drug Enforcement Admin)	
Professional Association Membership	
Malpractice Insurance	

Commercial Insurance	
Disability Insurance	
CME (Continuing Medical Education)	

CLINIC OPERATONAL FEES	**Fees vary**
CLIA (on-site Lab Cert. by State)	
Business license (City fee)	
Business license tax (City)	
Incorporation fee (State of VA)	
Board of Architectural Review (sign)	

OFFICE EQUIP/SUPPLIES	**Project an initial/ monthly expense**
Computer and software	
Fax/Copier	
Business Cards and Flyers	
Charts and paper supplies	
LEGAL/ACCOUNTING SUPPORT	**Project fees for start-up/ retaining**
Attorney	
CPA	

OFFICE STAFF EQUIPMENT	Project a dollar amount
2 Refrigerators (medication & food)	
Microwave	
Coffee Pot and Supplies	
Paper products	

DURABLE MEDICAL SUPPLIES	Project an annual dollar amount
Supplies	
Vaccinations: Td, Flu, PPD	

UTILITIES	Project an annual dollar amount
Electric	
Gas	
Water	
Telephone (land, cell, merchant)	

ADVERTISING	Project an annual dollar amount
Local newspaper	
Community telephone book	
Web site & Internet fee	
Postage	

OFFICE SUPPORT	Project an annual dollar amount
Supervising Physician	
Nurse/Medical Assistant/front end	
Owners Draw	

BIO-HAZARD	Project by monthly/ quarterly fee
Waste products	

Office Staff

Defining the office responsibilities of your staff is critical. Vague and undefined responsibility can cause staff to be lackadaisical and can create leftover duties for the owner. I learned that a written job description, including a list of duties, creates a productive office with very little confusion. This helps everyone to not only work better but "smarter," utilizing everyone's talents and assets to best advantage. You may not always agree with or like someone, but you can learn to work with him or her in a healthy work environment within established boundaries. In my clinic, all new staff and students sign a form similar to the confidentiality form to guarantee all patient information is not released or verbally shared with anyone in or outside the clinic who was not directly involved in the patients' care.

If you are a preceptor for a student, as I often am, it is always important to outline his or her role and duties. This direction allows the Nurse Practitioner or Physician Assistant student to attain his or her student objectives while fostering team spirit. I believe everyone, including students, wants to feel he or she is contributing to the success of a small business.

EMPLOYEE MANUAL
Mission Statement
HIPPA Policy
Hours of Operation of Clinic
Payroll Dates
Holidays
Health Plan, Retirement and 401K
Sick time, time off, emergency time off and vacation
Office Responsibilities/ Housekeeping Duties
Jury Duty
Preceptor Policy and Student Role
Grievance Policy
Disciplinary Action
Form for Staff Signature after review of Manual

Charts

Keeping charts accurate and up-to-date is critical. It is important that all patients have a good understanding of the clinic's policies and what their responsibilities are as patients.

CHART INSERTS
Clinic Policy and Procedures with Patient Signature
History of Patient with Patient Signature
Super bill and Insurance Policy with Patient Signature
HIPPA Policy with Patient Signature

Furniture and Office Equipment

As word spread that a neighborhood clinic was about to open, many closed medical offices donated equipment and furniture. I needed to store the furniture and equipment while the building was under construction. This became too costly, so I ended up moving all donated furniture, tables, chairs, and equipment into the clinic. The only medical equipment that I purchased was a nebulizer machine and a woods lamp. Initially, I leased an EKG machine and the merchant credit card terminal. As I paid off loans, and as the clinic grew, I purchased the EKG machine and the credit card terminal. It just did not seem logical and was not very cost efficient to continue leasing these items.

Internet Connection

Internet connectivity in a clinic has both a positive and negative impact on the productivity of your office staff and you. In the start-up costs of building the clinic, I did not have the funds to have Internet access so I used my personal home computer connection to the Internet for business needs. After seven years, I still do not have Internet access at the clinic. I rely on my home computer to access the Internet for business related issues. Honestly, I do not believe it would provide any more support than what is needed now. If the clinic grows in its staffing and providers, it may be a valuable tool for its office support. Presently it is still debatable.

The positive effect computer Internet access has for your clinic is multifaceted: it provides immediate contact with outside resources in gathering medical information to support symptoms related to accurate differential diagnoses. It also serves as a means to communicate with your patient. I do not feel comfortable relaying sensitive medical information over the telephone. For me it would be more difficult to do so over the Internet. If your business or clinic desires to communicate with your patients, the Internet is a good source for direct communication for medical questions and medical results. I still have my reservations about this form of communicating patient information, so in my opinion, "The jury is still out!"

It is also my opinion; the Internet is less personal and boasts a whole host of legal issues in regard to confidentiality and access to your patients email account. I am not privy to the legal-medial implications, for this type of vehicle. These are some of the questions you might want to pose, especially if you decide to offer Internet service to your patients. One very important concept is your ability to manage your time wisely. Will you be communicating more on the computer for the purpose of answering questions, versus seeing patients in the office? Will patients expect you to answer their questions without an office visit? Will your patients abuse their access to you via the Internet, and rely on this versus paying for an office visit? How and when will you establish boundaries ending this type of communicating, and start requiring an office visit? Can you charge for phone or Internet consultation? I do not have those answers. Again, these are some of the questions you may want to think about prior to offering this type of service to your patients.

Another positive value in having Internet access is the ability to order medication for your patients through the patient assistance program sponsored by various pharmaceutical companies. You can order and reorder medications are on the telephone or on the Internet. If you are able to order online, this saves precious time that is wasted being placed on telephone "hold." I would recommend having Internet access to communicate with other providers or facilities and conduct online research.

The negative implication of computer access is the opportunity for your staff to waste precious time on personal and Internet activities.

At times, I felt I needed to motivate many of my front-end staff; even after he or she was presented a detailed job description or task. Rather than organize charts or put together chart inserts, occasionally, I found my resourceful staff finding and playing games on my basic software package. I was unaware man of these games were included in the software package. I soon became very wise to this type of daily occurrence. Other issues you may encounter are personnel that might surf the Internet or participate in online activity un-related to daily work tasks.

Another reason computer access may be a concern for your clinic is the threat of confidential patient information being compromised. Factor the annual cost and risk of a compromised security into the purchase. I would have the extra concern that outside sources could access to information.

Computer Record and Chart System

There is something to be said about the ease of working on a computer. Many clinics and offices are still utilizing paper records. Albeit, it will only be a matter of time before it will be required to implement a computer software program for patient documentation. Transfer of records, sending referrals, and keeping permanent patient information is a part of moving into the future. This concept is two-fold; one is to keep your practice in line with technology and current trends in medical practice, but essentially, it may be a regulatory compliance issue that the federal government will require.

I am regularly reminded of an indecipherable note I once sent to my daughter's teacher. When my daughter came home, she stated, "My teacher could not read your writing, so I had to read your note to her!" Our profession has always been known as one that has almost illegible penmanship…need I say more! Clarity of good patient documentation will not only facilitate better patient communication but also allow for easy reading and better understanding of your patients' care and your recommendations.

Look for a software package that allows your office to easily implement patient documentation. If you are able, start your operation on a computer system. It will capacitate for more accurate transition in the future. There are also software packages that allow for discharge planning for patient care, and information that provides educational notes for better patient compliance of care.

Advertising And Marketing

As the clinic grew, so did the various options of marketing. Besides using the telephone book and word of mouth, others suggested I establish a Website for patients. The clinic had been opened almost two years before I launched a Website. My daughter created the initial page. Later I hired a computer expert to expand the site. This year a computer consultant assisted me with updating patient data, uploading a recent photo and added important components such as most frequently asked questions (FAQ).

The Queen Street Clinic Website is a useful vehicle for communicating valuable information: the mission statement, the location, the hours, policy, and most FAQs. It also includes a photo of me, the history of the clinic and photos of various patients who have been treated. When the photos were taken, I had all the patients sign model releases to allow their photos to be used on the clinic's website.

One exception to the information available on the Website is the listing of the fee for an office visit. I learned that is too expensive to frequently update the Website when prices change. This is also done to decrease the number of patients who challenge a pricing discrepancy. Durable medical supplies costs change frequently. On the page there was a disclaimer at the bottom of the fee for service page with a note that "Prices may vary." Price discrepancies were always a problem and that was resolved once the list was removed.

*The most important thing in any relationship
is not what you get, but what you give.*

— Eleanor Roosevelt

PART V

Prevent an Impasse

Insured versus Uninsured

Often a patient demands free care and does not understand the concept of *discounted* heath care. If you have never paid for health care, you may not understand how the health care system works. Those who are without health care coverage or who may no longer be eligible for public health assistance may feel taken advantage being charged for a medical office visit. Paying for an office visit is a foreign concept difficult for many patients to understand. In the past, these people have been accustomed to co-pays and not having to remit for an office visit. A frequent question posed is: "Why must I pay the full charge for an office visit or consultation?" This is when I sit down with the patient, take a history, ask why he or she needs to be seen, and gather information to make differential diagnoses. Years ago I learned that 90 percent of the patient's diagnosis is in the history-taking. Spending time with the patient is critical for assessing if laboratory, imaging, or office procedures need to be implemented.

Perhaps the greatest challenge is the notion that if you provide health care to those who are less fortunate, and charge a fee, you are not a genuinely caring person; you are taking what little money some have. Some insist that such a clinic is or should be "free." This misconception is probably one of the biggest challenges I had to overcome. It is very difficult to try to assess and manage a person's health care if the person will not pay for the laboratory work to support a diagnosis. It is also unfortunate that the idea of running a clinic as a small business is considered uncharitable and mercenary. I have potential patients say: "What kind of person are you to charge a fee? If you really cared about my medical condition, you wouldn't charge me anything."

Patients with insurance are often unaware of the "real costs" of procedural diagnostic tools, such as the expense of laboratory work or an MRI. The majority of Americans who have health insurance are completely unacquainted with the cost of testing and procedures. They fall primarily into the category of paying a monthly premium that is matched or supplemented by employers, along with nominal co-pay charged at the time of the office visit. Occasionally, patients with insurance and a regular provider visit the clinic because of inability to have an appointment as quickly as they prefer with the primary care physician. This group often questions a full charge of an office visit rather than the lower co-pay fee. Another misunderstanding is charges for add-on tests that the person never needed to pay previously. As stated before, the office visit fee and procedural testing are sometimes needed to determine a diagnosis and possibly write a prescription for a malady. Safe, prudent medical care is what keeps people healthy. On a daily basis I remind all patients I practice with diligence and competence. I'm not a magician! Many times procedural testing and imaging have to be ordered to make an accurate diagnosis.

Another group of patients are composed of those who previously had medical coverage with defunct insurance companies. At times, new insurance carriers will deny health care insurance as a result of a pre-existing condition. Now and again companies charge monthly fees too costly for the client to afford. Recently a gentleman came into the clinic and explained that his new carrier did not deny him coverage but required the payment of $1,900 for a single coverage monthly premium. He felt this was only the beginning of the price escalation he would incur and was happy to drop this coverage and enjoy the services of the clinic and its discounted fees.

I am not a member of any Health Maintenance Organization (HMO) or Preferred Provider Organization (PPO) plan, and I do not file insurance forms. Payment is strictly in cash or by credit card. Furthermore, my billing system is not set up for insurance and Current Procedural Terminology (CPT) coding. I encourage patients to use my Federal Tax ID number and super bill and submit the paperwork to their insurance companies. I have often had to defend these policies due to complaints brought to the attention of the city's Consumer Affairs Office from patients who, after their visits, attempt to file my super bill for reimbursement of charges. Though my super bill has my Federal Tax ID number on it, I do not have access to diagnoses codes for the purpose of patient reimbursement.

Scheduled Appointments and No-Show Policy

Often patients do not keep their scheduled appointments. This is the status quo for any practice or business. This creates many problems from staffing to revenue. Since I do not double book appointments, I assume the person who requests an appointment will arrive at the scheduled time. In the clinic policy, a no-show fee is stated. Because the clinic does not take insurance, it is difficult to recapture the loss in revenue for that time slot if the person does not show for his or her appointment. If this occurs with an established patient, I will put a note in his or her chart, and at the next visit I will attempt to collect the nominal fee for a "no-show."

One of my biggest frustrations is an early morning appointment that is not kept. Typically it is a patient who demands the first appointment of the day but who fails to arrive for his or her scheduled slot. I will admit that it can be irritating when I have rearranged my schedule to accommodate their needs. At times I say, "No more early morning appointments without a pre-payment!" I try to be consistent with this rule.

Another difficult clinic pattern is the occurrence of a patient or patients walk in without a scheduled appointment. Periodically, four or five patients arrive at the same time and demand to be seen immediately. This can be over his or her lunch hour or on a break. This can be overwhelming. The difficulty is when the patient is medically challenging, and I need to take a thorough history, while another patient walks up to the counter asking, "How much longer will it be until I can be seen?" I request patients make appointments so that I can anticipate arrival times. Much of my patient base does not understand I am not an urgent care and need adequate time to assess properly the medical condition.

Responding to Prejudices of a Culturally Diverse Population

As the clinic grew, I realized that it was vital for patients to understand its mission and the purpose for creating the clinic. The United States has a much different process in the delivery of health care than other countries around the world. Two concepts had to be reinforced to my culturally diverse patient population. First, health care is not free in the United States. Just because "clinic" is part of the operation's name does not necessarily mean that its services are free of charge. Secondly, it is not unusual for a woman to not only build but operate a medical practice in this country.

Catastrophic Insurance

I am frequently asked what type of medical insurance I would recommend for health care coverage. I do not have the answer to this question. I would strongly encourage anyone who asks that question to investigate the various plans that include emergency hospitalizations. It is my understanding that there are many plans that provide coverage for catastrophic events. This type of coverage would be especially important in the event of an accident with subsequent immediate hospitalization. Having catastrophic insurance is coverage that many have, though they have not made the decision to carry traditional medical health care insurance due to the high monthly premiums.

I have also noticed a trend among those people who are self-employed. Those independents face the difficulty of not being able to buy into group plans. Often, if they are able to acquire the medical health care coverage, it is extremely expensive. Many who are self-employed only carry a plan that covers catastrophic events. These plans vary in price and can be affordable and provide the person peace of mind. No one wants to be in a position where an illness or accident causes him or her to incur a large hospital bill after a catastrophic medical event or malady.

Moving into the Future:
The Supermarket Clinic

Where is health care taking us? As we move forward into the future, I am very concerned with urgent clinics that are popping up in the strip malls, super centers, drug stores, and supermarkets. I think this concept offers a variety of sites to use for non-emergent care. I am concerned that in the long term, these clinics fall short in delivering primary care, follow-up care, and the necessary referrals to specialists.

I am not opposed to this new trend in providing a medical service. In fact, I consulted for one corporation interested in promoting development and growth of similar facilities. I consulted during a two-day training session, describing my business and the strengths and weaknesses of being a sole provider. This corporation was planning to expand its supermarket clinics into other cities and outlying states. I enjoyed visiting this site but had a few questions about the facility's approach to patient assessment. I was concerned about the absence of an examination table, the limitation of examination tools (e.g., laboratory services) and minimal patient privacy. Not having an examination table limits ability to perform a full examination. I also questioned the location of their charts and method for tracking patients for follow-up care or referrals. None of these questions had been addressed. I also noticed they were hiring Nurse Practitioners from areas outside the community where they were opening the clinics. The question I posed was: Why were they hiring Nurse Practitioners from across the United States when they should have been hiring professional who were familiar with the resources in the respective community? Marketing the concept of a clinic in a large retail space requires knowledge of the community. This knowledge is priceless, and knowing your community and its leaders is one very important element in establishing an outreach program and plan.

I was also interested if the corporation had a "non-compete" policy or employment contract. As more supermarket clinics open, I would want to make certain when hiring a Nurse Practitioner what he or she expected in terms of ownership. I would not want to invest time, money and training if this person is likely to leave and seek employment elsewhere. First of all, it may not have been a good fit. There may be other reasons, and I would not want someone taking the corporation's ideas and concepts and seeking employment elsewhere.

I am not trying to dismiss the value of the supermarket clinic, but I do believe these clinics need to look at and focus on the long-term care and follow-up care provided to the patients. Many of these clinics will accept insurance and are a great option to the long waits in the hospital emergency room. I am hopeful the staff is prepared to discuss other health care issues that may need to be addressed. In essence, these supermarket clinics may be an after-hour "quick fix" or a "band-aid" until patients can be seen by their primary care provider.

People who do not have insurance will again fall in between the cracks. These non-insured patients may again fail to have a follow up appointment and repeat this type of clinic visit when feeling poorly. Patterns as these are a result of how so many individuals wait until too ill or a chronic illness lands them into the hospital. I frequently treat patients who insist on not having laboratory work secondary to an acute illness. Some, who agree to have these tests run, have high blood sugar and require hospitalization. If the patient had been seen regularly in a medical home or a clinic, this diagnosis may have been discovered prior to emergent hospitalization. Not only does a crisis situation like this become very costly, but these individuals many times cannot pay the hospital bill. Compounding the tragedy may be loss of wages or — worse — loss of employment. From experience, I know that the phrase, "An ounce of prevention is worth a pound of cure" (*Benjamin Franklin*) has a lot of truth.

I am often curious if these supermarket clinics would welcome partnering with a model much like the Queen Street Clinic for those who are medically uninsured. This would provide those who are medically uninsured receive follow-up care and also ensure adequate primary care is available.

Not-for-Profit Status versus a Small Business

I decided not to seek nonprofit status for the clinic. My mission statement clearly defines what the goals and objectives of the clinic are and describes why it was built. Being a privately-owned small business does not allow the clinic to receive the funds of local, state, and federal government or grant money. Occasionally, the clinic receives private donations.

Nonprofits require governance by appointed board members who may or may not be fully invested in the life or success of such an operation. Board members must actively solicit grant money and participate in the grant-writing process. Furthermore, board members may intentionally or unintentionally meddle in the day-to-day operations of the clinic, compromising its independence. It is disingenuous to restructure a privately-owned clinic — built with the personal funds and sweat equity of the building's owner — to a not-for-profit entity.

At one point The Queen Street Clinic had a non-profit status. The burden of being the sole medical provider and the executive director can be to be overwhelming because I see patients all day and am expected to write grants in the evening. The fear of failure and the loss of my business and home are ever-present on my mind. My financial priority is to replenish the personal funds used and remove the lien on my home. After all, I established the clinic to extend health care to the medically uninsured, not to host monthly board meeting dinners to review the operational status of a nonprofit clinic! One day I reflected on the clinic's new nonprofit status and realized that I was not being true to the mission statement and goals of the business.

I am not opposed to clinics operating under a not-for-profit status. It was not a comfortable fit for my model of health care delivery in its infancy. If the clinic had remained as a nonprofit, regular fundraisers would have been held. I have always wanted to have a fundraiser but as yet have not found the time to organize one. Orchestrating a fundraiser would be a wonderful task for a partner who could promote and market the concept of the clinic. I truly believe if more people were aware of the work being done at the clinic there would be more enthusiasm and community involvement.

The lesson to be learned in this business detour is that if you wish to establish your clinic as a nonprofit, first secure funds from a philanthropist or grant sources and do not use your personal funds. Additionally, I had proved that people are willing to pay a nominal fee when good health care is competent, accessible and affordable. If the fee is fair and the delivery of care is competent, the patient will return.

The Importance of Accuracy and Compliance

Many patients do not understand the concept of accurately completing a form designed by another facility, such as a school or entrance into a health care field. Many times patients arrive with school and sports physicals and for each there are specific requirements stated on the particular form. This is confusing. When a health care provider signs a form, the provider is stating that all the documented information on the form is correct and recorded with the intention to screen the patient for health care problems. Examples of such screening include hematocrit and lead serum testing. Additionally a urinalysis is usually part of the physical and the aforementioned testing is not free of charge. Sometimes the forms include immunizations be up-to-date and titers be drawn for measles, mumps and rubella (MMR) or varicella.

Ever so often patients argue they need not comply with having these tests done. Being consistent and listing prices will usually preclude this discussion. If the state requirements are identified on the form, this can help diffuse an argument. Many times you need to state these are not requirements of the clinic, but a book to follow for the completion of the form, and there are added costs due to the form requirements.

Consistency and telling the patient it is illegal to sign a form without completing the requirements is a challenge. Such a clinic policy should not be undermined by angry patients who feel they are being overcharged. Simply state that it is the law, and that the practitioner's license and his or her ethical and professional integrity are at stake.

When Complaints Result in Investigations

I would be remiss if I did not address the issue of complaints made by patients. It is unfortunate that no matter how hard your office staff and you as the practitioner attempt to meet the needs of your patients there will be complaints made to the Department of Health. It appears to be a pattern with patients who will challenge the effort of the clinic staff. This can be difficult and sometimes very embarrassing to have formal charges made regarding your practice style or what is considered safe and prudent care. The Board of Health has an obligation to investigate all accusations that are made regardless of their merit, truth, or fact. It can be exhausting and frustrating having to reply to a charge that is unfounded and inaccurate. Such obligations come with the territory of being an owner. It is my opinion if safe and prudent health care is delivered with honesty and sincerity you cannot be faulted for your care. Present the facts and keep good documentation if you feel that a complaint will result in an investigation.

Other challenges arise from patients using merchant charge cards for care, and dispute the services already provided or agreed to with the provider. This, too, is exhausting because you must reply to defend the services rendered so your practice does not forfeit the money owed. Displaying a clear fee policy at the front desk, and having a clinic policy form signed by the patient in his or her chart is as much as your practice can do. Taking these precautions is the only way to prevent patients from canceling their credit card charges for services already rendered. The clinic's copy of the merchant charge slip should clearly state, "All SALES FINAL. ABSOLUTELY NO REFUNDS! INCLUDING OFFICE VISITS, OFFICE TESTING AND AGREED TO LAB DRAWS."

Far better is, to dare might things,
To win glorious triumphs,
Even though checkered by failure
Than to rank with those poor spirits who
Neither enjoy much nor suffer much,
Because they live in the grey
Twilight that knows neither victory nor defeat

- Theodore Roosevelt

PART VI

THE QUEEN STREET CLINIC

Photography of Clinic

circa: September 2000
The exterior of the front of the building before it was purchased.

circa: September 2000

A side profile of the building before it was purchased.

circa: April 2001
Junk found in the basement of the building.

circa: June 2001

Inside the building, prior to the renovation of the downstairs, this space would become the lobby and reception area.

circa: June 2001

The upstairs of the building, the ceiling and roof are gone, this would become one of the rooms that would be renovated into an examination room.

circa: June 2001

The lobby being renovated and more junk that came out of the basement.

circa: June 2001

Another upstairs room that was renovated into a office area. Under the linen are pieces of furniture that were collected to fill the clinic. The ceiling is in need of much repair.

circa: June 2001

The lobby, looking out of the building. The windows and doors had steel bars in place.

circa: June 2001

The downstairs of the building, looking from the back of the building towards the lobby. An examination table and crutches waiting to be used.

circa: July 2001

The exterior of the clinic, after the renovation of the building. The clinic signs are installed and the name of the clinic has been added to a new door. The bars are gone from the windows and the door.

circa: July 2001

The outside clinic sign has been hung. The sign had to meet the approval of the Board of Architectural Review of Alexandria. The clinic is located in one of the historic areas of Old Town, Alexandria, called Parker-Gray.

circa: August 2001

The clinic is open for business. In the lobby an antique hutch that holds historic medical instruments and items that were collected for display. Patients love to look inside.

circa: August 2001

The lobby of the clinic after it has been renovated. The clinic is now open for business. The antique chairs were donated by a former physician who practiced in Alexandria.

circa: August 2001

The back of the clinic and triage area after the renovation. The checkerboard tile floor that follows the vintage appearance of the clinic.

circa: August 2001

Remember the prior photograph of an upstairs examination room, prior to the renovation, it is now ready to be used for patient examination.

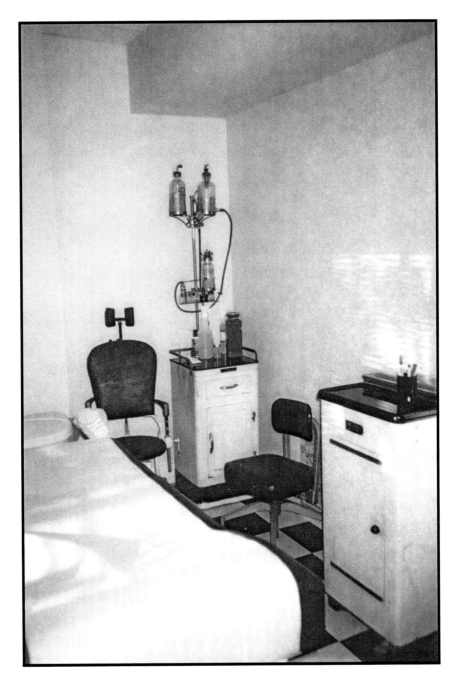

circa: August 2001
Another view of the same room, ready to be used for patient care.

Photograph by Allison Silberberg

circa: April 2004

Three very special patients who are frequently seen at the clinic with Anne Boston Parish

My friend, James Earl Parker...

Photograph by Allison Silberberg

circa: April 2004

Just to have a decent conversation with you is a blessing, 'cause you can tell people something that they can benefit from.
You are my angel.
— James Earl Parker

Life affords no greater responsibility, no greater privilege, than the raising of the next generation.

— C. Everett Koop

Queen Street Clinic, PLC Mission Statement

Queen Street Clinic, PLC is a private medical practice intending to provide affordable, compassionate, quality healthcare to the medically uninsured. The Clinic was built out of the private funds of the founder/owner. It is not a free clinic and does not accept any form of insurance, including Medicare or Medicaid. The clinic provides treatment to people of all ages and ethnic backgrounds with a specific focus on management of chronic disease, prevention of illness, and health education. By improving the healthcare management of the uninsured community, the long term adverse effects associated with untreated medical conditions will be markedly diminished. Through partnerships with laboratory facilities, imaging centers and local medical specialists the clinic strives to provide a comprehensive range of affordable medical services.

Queen Street Clinic Price Menu

*prices may vary due to the constant change in medical cost; not all service prices are listed.

Welcome! This clinic <u>is not a free clinic</u>, nor do we accept insurance. What we do provide is discounted health care for the medically uninsured.

OFFICE VISIT...$60.00

*This includes a complete history, physical exam, patient education, and written prescription if needed.

LABORATORY EXAMS..$90.00

*Average price for <u>most</u> individual blood/serum exams although <u>not all</u> exams, pending the method of investigation and procedure.

WELL WOMAN EXAM $240.00

*Includes complete history, physical exam with breast exam, and PAP smear with result reading. Also cultures for bacterial vaginosis or yeast if needed and a prescription for medications and counseling if needed. If PAP results are abnormal there are two options for resolution. One, an office visit ($60.00) to discuss results, provide education and possible medication with repeat PAP in 2-3 months. Second, an office visit for education and a referral letter to a specialist for an evaluation of a possible colposcopy and/ or biopsy.

STD TESTING....................................PRICES MAY VARY

STD testing for herpes, Chlamydia, Gonorrhea, HPV, HIV, and Syphilis are additional charges and can be discussed in the office visit as needed.

MAMMOGRAM..$40.00

*Evaluation and reading of exam. If you live in Alexandria proper you qualify for a free exam.

SCHOOL PHYSICAL... $145.00

*Includes complete history, physical exam required by school, hearing exam, vision screening, urinalysis, hematocrit (blood test), and TB skin test. If lead test is required there is an additional $40.00 fee (<6 y.o.)

DOT PHYSICAL..$175.00

*Includes complete history, physical exam required by employer, vision screening, and urinalysis.

TB SKIN TEST..$35.00

*Includes inoculation and read 48-72 hours later, this does not include the required office visit of $60.00. If you fail to show for skin read you must pay for another TB test. If test is positive, we are required to order a chest x-ray which is an additional cost of $40.00.

RAPID STREP TEST.. **$115.00**

*Includes swab of throat and results of test within 5 minutes. This does not include the $60.00 required office visit.

ECG **$155.00**

*Includes a 12-lead evaluation and result interpretation by Licensed Nurse Practitioner.

XRAY.. **$40.00**

*Fee per view

REFERRAL TO SPECIALIST **$120.00**

*Includes a typed letter that contains all pertinent information (i.e. lab results, x-ray evaluations, medications, historical information, etc.) required by the specialist for a proper examination. Does not include the specialist's office visit fee.

COPIES OF CHART CONTENTS **$1.00/page**

*Requires a 15 day advance notice and payment up front.

Example of a Typical Chronic Illness Situation

"I used to receive care from a local facility but I no longer qualify (i.e. am ineligible or residency status has changed) for care in this system. I have had diabetes and hypertension for a few years now and only need my medications refilled."

In order to provide proper quality health care for this individual we would be required take a full medical history, physical examination, and order the proper lab work to confirm this diagnosis and prescribe the correct dose of medication. The labs are to ensure that medications are dosed at the proper levels, as well checking to see if the vital organs involved are in good health. This type of visit would require;

Office visit – $60.00

Labs – $90.00/each

> Hemoglobin A1c (glucose level maintenance over 3 months)
> Basic Metabolic Panel (kidney function)
> Hepatic function Panel (liver function)
> Lipid panel (cholesterol levels)
> Total cost $420.00*

Average cost at another facility in local area:

Office visit – $140.00

Labs – $105.00 (for all 4)

Lab draw – $20.00

Total cost $570.00

*Please remember that in order to properly care for this type of patient in the future, periodic follow-up visits and lab tests will be required. This ensures the patient's health is managed properly and safely so that this person can live a quality life with diabetes.

Queen Street Clinic Payment Policy

- A CHARGE OF $60.00 IS REQUIRED FOR AN OFFICE VISIT BEFORE BEING SEEN.

- LAB TESTS AND X-RAYS AND/OR IMAGING ARE NOT INCLUDED IN THE $60.00 CHARGE.

- ALL LAB CHARGES ARE PAID AT THE TIME OF THE OFFICE VISIT. THESE CHARGES ARE NON-REFUNDABLE.

- IT MAY BE REQUIRED THAT LAB TESTS BE ORDERED TO ASSESS AN INFECTION OR CHRONIC ILLNESS.

- TO PICK UP A PRESCRIPTION BASED ON ABNORMAL LAB RESULTS THERE IS AN OFFICE FEE OF $60.00 FOR PATIENT EDUCATION.

- ALL X-RAYS AND IMAGING CHARGES ARE PAID AT THE SITE WHERE THE X-RAY OR IMAGING WILL BE PERFORMED.

- $20.00 WILL BE CHARGED FOR A MISSED APPOINTMENT; WITHOUT PRIOR CANCELA-TION.

- NO EXCEPTIONS TO THESE POLICIES!

More Clinic Policy

- THE BATHROOM IS FOR PATIENTS ONLY
- NO EATING OR DRINKING IN THE LOBBY
- THE CLINIC TELEPHONE IS FOR STAFF ONLY
- CHILDREN ARE NOT ALLOWED IN THE CLINIC UNLESS THEY ARE PATIENTS; THIS TO PROTECT THEM FROM EXPOSURE TO ILLNESS AND DISEASE
- I RESERVE THE RIGHT TO REFUSE MEDICAL SERVICES TO ANYONE WHO IS ABUSIVE TO STAFF AND THE PROVIDER. WHETHER PATIENT, SPOUSE, COMPANION, PARENT, RELATIVE OR CAREGIVER

Clinic Rules

QUEEN STREET CLINIC IS NOT FREE!

QUEEN STREET CLINIC DOES NOT ACCEPT MEDICAID, MEDICARE OR INSURANCE!

PAYMENT IS TAKEN PRIOR TO THE OFFICE VISIT!

MRI, CT SCANS, IMAGING AND LAB WORK ARE NOT INCLUDED IN THE $60.00 OFFICE VISIT!

QUEEN STREET CLINIC DOES NOT HAVE A MEMBERSHIP; THE $60.00 OFFICE VISIT IS NOT A ONE TIME ONLY FEE!

NO REFUNDS FOR AGREED-TO LAB WORK OR OFFICE VISITS!

ADDITIONAL LAB WORK OR IMAGING MAY BE REQUIRED FOR DIAGNOSING AN ILLNESS!

DEMANDING PRESCRIPTIONS IS NOT ACCEPTABLE!

NO SMOKING IN THE CLINIC!

NO EATING OR DRINKING IN THE CLINIC!

NO CELL PHONE USE IN THE CLINIC!

THE BATHROOM IS ONLY FOR CLINIC PATIENTS!

CHILDREN ARE NOT ALLOWED IN THE CLINIC UNLESS THEY ARE BEING SEEN! THIS IS TO PROTECT THEM FROM CATCHING DISEASE AND ILLNESS!

DO NOT LET YOUR CHILD JUMP ON THE CHAIRS, WRITE ON THE WALLS, THROW TOYS, OR URINATE IN THE CORNERS!

WALK IN APPOINTMENTS WILL BE SEEN IN THE ORDER THEY WALK IN!

A FEE WILL BE CHARGED FOR A "NO SHOW!

NO FAXING OR COPYING WITHOUT PRE-PAYMENT!

YELLING AT THE PROVIDER IS NOT ALLOWED

Do not go where the path may lead,
Go instead where there is no path and leave a
trail.

- Ralph Waldo Emerson

PART VII

CASE STUDIES

The case studies are to provide some answers to the most frequently asked questions. There are many days that I receive telephone calls from other Nurse Practitioners or non-medical individuals who want to know: "How did you get started?" Well, I learned to say.... Do you have a few hours? I have put together some case studies and some lessons that were learned through "Baptism by Fire!" I have tried to personalize the studies in a storytelling format that reinforces the elements found throughout the book.

CASE #1 -

Sole Provider in a Specialty Practice

This case study examines the pros and cons of a single provider and her ability to restructure her practice and increase her patient volume while operating a women's clinic in her community "Her Own Way".

"Nancy"

One afternoon I received a telephone call from Nancy, a Nurse Practitioner who specializes in Woman's Health. She had read about my practice in one of the articles that had been published about the Queen Street Clinic. Nancy was interested in "how to" restructure her clinic to become more profitable. She was renting an office space that only included one examination room, and she only wanted to work two days per week. She was very excited about my success and wanted to seek my opinion about how I was able to sustain my practice as my patient volume grew. I asked Nancy if she had completed a market analysis of her community to identify the group of women that she wished to capture. She had not done so. She had always wanted to pursue "her own way" to provide health care. After reading about the Queen Street Clinic, she became excited that "she too" could open her own practice.

I asked her about her expected volume, the time she wanted to allot to each patient and the atmosphere in the office space. She said that, "I only wanted to see one to three patients a day." I then asked her how she was to maintain her overhead with so little volume and how she could support the "silent" or indirect costs and expenses that go hand in hand with a small business. Nancy felt that providing a warm and friendly waiting area would generate the growth of her patient base. Nancy also said she would be serving tea and cookies while her patients were filling out the paperwork and waiting to be seen. I questioned Nancy about her added cost by offering tea and cookies. She felt it would provide a cozy and warm office atmosphere and this would attach a strong patient base and following.

Since that time, I have spoken to Nancy and discovered she was not able to sustain her practice. Nancy felt this was secondary to the added costs that far exceeded her ability to pay the rent and sustain her operational budget. Nancy has returned to providing care in a family practice in her home town and will continue to rethink her future option to operate her own practice.

The Lessons to be Learned

If Nancy had a partner or second provider, she may have been able to absorb the added costs, because this second provider could recapture the revenue for the cookies and tea in the office. Though cookies and tea may represent a minimal expense, silent costs do add up. Of course the other silent costs would have been for her durable medical supplies; utilities (if her rent did not include utilities) and any other costs that she needed to absorb to open a practice.

With a second provider, Nancy would be able to manage the marketing aspect of increasing her patient volume. Additionally this would allow her the available time needed to market her unique concept in the community. During this time, the second provider may treat patients with generated revenue from the practice. While providing a warm and friendly atmosphere in the waiting room is a wonderful idea, most patients do not expect to receive beverages and food while waiting to see a provider.

In their start-up phase, most practices are mindful of every cent and dollar earned and spent. I applaud Nancy's aspiration in to provide the tea and cookies service, but I believe most patients are content just getting seen on time. It is an attractive thought, but unnecessary services can add up financially in the long run. Another viewpoint would be from those people who might ask why the office could not charge less for an office visit and not offer the food and beverage.

Patients are usually able to identify charges related to their care and how they may be a reflection of hidden costs they are not willing to absorb. I could hear the words echoed, "So can I pay only $55 dollars instead of $60 dollars for an office visit since I did not eat your cookies or drink your beverage?

As Nancy's practice grew, in my opinion, she might be able to offer this wonderful amenity once she recovered her start-up costs and the patient volume grew and the practice started generating revenue. Nancy really needed to look at the bottom line and focus on finding someone else to facilitate patient care and spur marketing efforts.

Some examples of effective outreach that would help expand her practice might include the following:

- providing free evening educational seminars that focused on women's health
- buying tables at school fairs, country health screening fairs and area social group gatherings
- printing and distributing marketing coupons that could be purchased as a gift to give as an "expression of love" to employees, nannies, babysitters, housekeepers and anyone who may be working in a   service-oriented occupation

and may not have the benefit of health care insurance or a medical home.

When I initially spoke to Nancy I inquired if she had done a market analysis of her community needs. She had not done this piece of her organizational start-up. Such a survey would have given her the opportunity to have a level of comfort that her concept would support the new start of a clinic specifically focused on the medical needs of women. I remember having done a market analysis of Alexandria, and was able to identity that there were 24,000 medically uninsured residents in the city alone. This, of course, did not include the people in the outlying communities who would be able to use the clinic. In retrospect, Nancy should have taken a serious look at the community and the existing women heath clinics or practices. Only then would she have known if her community could support another women's specialty practice.

Renting verses purchasing an office space can be a huge decision when you make that leap to operate your own practice. When Nancy decided to rent space, she negotiated a month-to-month contract. This allowed her the opportunity to regularly evaluate the growth and progress of her practice. This also allowed her the opportunity to terminate the contract, if necessary, within a month. Many times renting space can be a frugal way to begin a practice. If you have the opportunity and the revenue to purchase a work space that, too, would be a good option. But Nancy's decision to rent space was a wise one given the unpredictable outlook of the clinic's long-term success along with not having a good sense of her patient base and income.

One last thought regarding operational costs. Capital costs that usually exceed $500 can be very difficult to absorb with the start-up costs of a medical practice. Renting an office space that comes furnished with equipment such as examination tables and desks can be a great way not to have to absorb those early purchases. This is especially true if you are not sure you will be open a year from your first anniversary. For Nancy this proved to be the right way to start her business; especially when she made the decision to return to a family practice. She did not have to incur those costs, and she only had to terminate her rental agreement for the office space. Even renting office equipment such as a merchant terminal or fax machine can be very economical in the beginning. If the practice continues to grow, purchasing these items would prove to be a good investment. Purchasing the equipment also eliminates the monthly rental fee and associated interest charges. Some might argue this is part of operational costs and an accountant may advise you differently. In my opinion, it is just one less monthly bill that needs to be paid.

CASE # 2 -
Health Care Screening

This case study discusses a Nurse Practitioner and his collaboration with his church and the positive outcome for the delivery of health care screening.

"Donald"

Donald was an energetic middle-age man who had chosen a career change and recently completed a nurse practitioner program. He was working full time for a medical practice, but he was enthusiastic and very interested in setting up a clinic in his neighborhood church rectory. He wanted to know how to begin a realistic plan to provide health screenings after weekly church services. He called me to inquire about the requirements to establish an outreach health screening clinic.

I asked him how he would fund the equipment and supplies that are needed for the screening. I also asked him how often he planned to offer the screening. Was he going to charge the patient or would the screening be free? Donald was delighted to offer his skills and knowledge as a Nurse Practitioner for free, and he thought his church would be willing to fund the other costs. He had spoken to the Parish Council and its members were supportive. This sounded great, and I was thrilled for him. He would have some assistance with the start-up costs for supplies and laboratory charges. I asked him about the church's commitment to assisting him financially. It was important for Donald to know what funds were available. Was the funding limited, or would the funding be unrestricted? I asked Donald to be mindful of start-up costs and to be aware of "silent costs" aside from the costs of renting or purchasing equipment to support his screening efforts. I then asked Donald if he had a plan for patient follow-up care. If he were to find an abnormal laboratory test, how would he pass the information to the patient? Must he have a referral plan established for care of the abnormal laboratory value?

Additionally I asked him what state he would practice in, and if he would need a collaborating or supervising physician regarding state requirements. I only mentioned this because each state has varying degrees of physician supervision and or collaborative practice. Additionally, he needed to be mindful of the Clinical Laboratory Improvement Amendments (CLIA) requirements. I also mentioned his need for malpractice insurance and how it would fit into his plan.

Donald felt the church would assist him with the start-up costs, and he thought he might be able to amass church donations to purchase the equipment and fund the laboratory charges. Donald and I spoke over the next few months, and although he knew that such a church-based clinic was very much needed, he could not devote the time needed to adequately provide the screening, the review of laboratory results and the final step of following up with the results of screenings and referrals to specialists.

Donald resided in a state that required collaboration and supervision for his health care efforts. He approached one of his fellow parishioners, who was a physician, and asked him to work with him under a practice agreement. He agreed to function in the role of his supervising physician but was only willing to offer a few hours monthly. Donald had not anticipated the scope of weekly patient intervention and screening and the follow-up of laboratory results that had been ordered. I asked him about his willingness to make telephone calls and be available for counseling. He had not anticipated that he would have to devote such long hours to follow-up care and referrals.

Donald rethought his plan and decided to volunteer at a community Free Clinic. He reorganized his concept and concluded that he could not support the time and costs by himself — even with the support of the church. The idea was too large for one person who operated in a volunteer capacity. He truly believed his services would be invaluable at the local Free Clinic. Donald decided to post flyers and use the church bulletin as a vehicle to circulate information about free health screening provided by the community Free Clinic at which he now volunteered.

The Lessons to be Learned

Start-up costs can be overwhelming. Donald was fortunate that the church offered him a room to use as an office for his health care screening. This was truly a blessing because the "silent costs" of rent, electricity, gas and water can be expensive. Cleaning services and paper products can also be costly. Donald was fortunate because he was offered the office at no charge and the facilities to support an office. Costs for paper and supplies to support the creation of patient reports or charts need to be factored into his overhead as well. Even with the church willingness to use the photocopy machine and telephone, chart supplies can be expensive.

Effective health care providers maintain detailed patient histories — a key factor in making differential diagnoses. Donald should have a chart for screenings and any laboratory tests that are ordered on each patient. He also needs to secure the patient chart. HIPPA mandates that patient information needs to be in a secure place. Donald needed to find a secure site to store charts. My suggestion was to either have a locked cabinet at the church or to rent a storage shed. The cost of renting a storage shed proved to be more than he wanted absorb.

Time is critical in any operation, and in most medical practices or clinics there is usually time allotted for the provider to review his or her ordered laboratory results. Many practices have a support staff that notifies the patient that a follow-up visit is needed. I truly believe Donald's concept was genuine, but he was not mindful of the amount of time required for follow-up care and referrals of those with abnormal laboratory work. He also needed to account for time spent with his supervising physician. Many times review of laboratory work can amount to hours, especially if the patient volume is high.

After I emphasized the amount of time needed to review laboratory results, I reiterated the importance of his responsibility to relay this information back to the patient. Would he make a telephone call, or would he send a letter? Would Donald be able to track this person and give the results to him or her? The time element was the factor that convinced him that his efforts would be better served at a Free Community Clinic.

CASE # 3 -
Administrative Hurdles

This case study involves many of the routine administrative duties that the office and the medical staff perform.

"Alice" and "Meg"

One afternoon following a difficult confrontation with one of my patients I received a telephone call from Alice, a Nurse Practitioner, who operated a practice in partnership with another Nurse Practitioner. They were experiencing some problems handling difficult patients at the time the patient signed in with the receptionist. I asked Alice how they handled the front-end interaction of their practice. Were patients greeted by a receptionist or nurse? Meg, a young but tough person, was the front-end receptionist. In many ways she was the prefect receptionist. She greeted each patient with a smile, respect and kindness as they entered the office. She addressed them in a friendly, respectful manner, asking them how they and their families were and how they were spending their days.

Daily, Meg faced patients who would argue over the up-front charge of an office visit and the supporting laboratory work. She soon began to burn out and stated, "As I entered the practice, a knot in my stomach would form knowing I may have a day filled with patients who would be difficult and upsetting, not only to me but to others who witnessed arguments over pre-payment of laboratory tests."

After I suggested that the practice create a list of charges that Meg could refer to, she felt less stressed and more relaxed as she greeted the clinic patients. She was reassured that the clinic policy clearly stated the terms of the medical management and that it would be enforceable. This, in turn, seemed to deceased the arguments that she had previously encountered.

Meg had a list of various diagnoses for patients who came in for chronic illness office visits. She knew that some laboratory tests were to be ordered every three months. She was instructed to let the patient know that the Nurse Practitioner wanted the laboratory tests ordered to assess his or her overall health and to evaluate if he or she was responding to the prescribed medication. I told Meg that she may encounter patients who demanded to see the provider before payment, but that she needed to reinforce that these were the established guidelines and let the patient know that the Nurse Practitioner had established these policies.

So why was Meg, with all her personality and friendliness, encountering so much difficulty with the collection of money needed to support the office visit and the required tests? This practice was experiencing some of the same difficulties that I encountered, such as patients who only wanted to pay for an office visit and a prescription but did not want to pay for the added fees of laboratory work to support their diagnoses.

Additionally, Meg would find herself confronted by a difficult patient who would demand that forms be completed without regard to medical requirements and state law. This was not new news to my practice; because I, too, had experienced patients only wanting signatures without any regard to compliance with these forms. My suggestion was to show the patient the form and explain that these tests were required by the state before the Nurse Practitioner could sign the form.

Another factor that seemed to cause a problem was the cultural aspect in providing health care for the patients who were foreign born. Many of the patients who used the clinic did not fully understand the forms that they were asked to complete for school or employment. Meg did not speak a foreign language, and many patients would come into the clinic without an interpreter, which limited Meg's ability to communicate and made her job that much more difficult. For others, who spoke a language, other then Spanish, there did not seem to be a translation problem, because they usually were brought in by a family member who would help bridge the language barrier by translating for the patient.

The cultural component can be a huge hurdle to overcome and can be frustrating for both the patient as well as the office staff. Overcoming a language barrier takes time and frequently requires lengthy explanations that can be exhausting for one person. My suggestion would be for Meg to either learn Spanish — since she stated that one-third of their patient base was Hispanic — or for the clinic to hire another part-time or full-time receptionist who spoke Spanish (provided there were operational funds to support another front end receptionist).

The Lessons to be Learned
One of the first questions I am frequently asked is how do I find the right mix of staff for my clinic? This is a good question, because it is sometimes difficult to find an effective gatekeeper or receptionist for your front desk. This person or persons are the cornerstones in the growth and success of your practice. I have learned that you

cannot motivate people to perform and that is a tough lesson to learn. My sense of finding the right mix is to allow the person to work for a few days without being paid. This allows you to evaluate their work ethic and evaluate if your clinic's work environment is a good fit for the prospective employee. It will also let you see if their personality is compatible with yours. Sometimes it takes more then a few days to assess the work ethic of a new hire.

Having an Employee Manual as a reference guide provides some direction for the new hire and a detailed job description helps to clarify his or her duties. The second part of hiring staff is guiding students. Many times you may be asked to precept students. This, too, can be a difficult task. Assessing students and providing an educational environment can be a challenge. You may find that not all students are a good fit for the type of entrepreneurial business model that your medical practice represents. They may want a more restricted range of duties that is typical of a larger practice. For instance, they may feel their role is only to see patients. In a small practice one wears many hats and the student needs to understand that picking up a telephone receiver and scheduling an appointment is a small but integral part of clinic work.

I suggested that the office design a medical office policy form and have the patient sign it on his or her first visit. I also told Meg that she should enforce these policies and ensure that patients sign the form, which signifies that they are in agreement with them. I also told her she should enforce the clinic policy that had been written by the medical staff to monitor the health of each patient.

The policy would clearly state that the fee for the office visit did not include charges for laboratory work or imaging. Additionally, Meg should reinforce that the clinic had a no refund policy, and after the patient had agreed to the laboratory work and office visit they were to comply with the agreement.

Having a policy in which the patient pre-paid prevented loss of revenue. This was my suggestion after having experienced a patient walk out of my clinic after being treated for a laceration and being provided a tetanus shot. This was a cost that the clinic had to absorb. Having a list of charges available for inspection and pre-paying prevents someone from leaving without remitting for services performed.

Some patients can be challenging when it involves payment for laboratory work to support their diagnosis. So, I suggested they use the approach that most medical offices/practices/clinics use and that is to require laboratory testing to ensure the course of therapy was indeed appropriate, prudent and safe. I also emphasized to Meg that many patients had to be instructed that the clinic was not a pharmacy. Meg was also encouraged to state that the Nurse Practitioners may need laboratory work to support her assessment. She also was told to let the patient know that laboratory work was to ensure that the medication the patient was prescribed was managing his or her condition appropriately. This was especially a concern with the diabetic or the hypertensive patient.

CASE #4 -
Medical Termination of Patient Care

This particular case study focuses on the termination of a difficult patient. He had a history of challenging me about ordered laboratory work and at times became very verbally abusive He had multiple medical problems and was always noncompliant with follow-up care.

"Mr. G."

He admittedly stated that he could not secure a provider to follow his difficult medical management; and he was so grateful that I would work with him. Despite his sincere compliment, I tried to work with him and after five months; I had to send him the following letter of medical termination.

One month after he had been sent his letter of medical termination, he attempted to file a dispute with his merchant credit card account challenging the fact that he received services for his last office visit and resulting laboratory work. Both allegations were untrue.

Recently Mr. "G" attempted to re-enter the clinic. "Are we cool?" he asked. I explained that the certified letter that he received explained he would have to find a new provider. I told him that his medication had been sent back to the pharmaceutical company and that he should receive it from another provider. He replied angrily, "There are no other providers in Alexandria who will see me!"

When he left I had a feeling this was not going to be the last time I would hear from him.

Mr. G.

1 Nowhere

Alexandria, Virginia

22314

August 10, 2007   **Delivered: Certified Mail**

Reference: Termination of Medical Care

Dear Mr. G:

This letter is to notify you that effective September 10, 2007 I will no longer be available to provide health care needs for you. As you know, I have been your provider since March 2, 2007; however you will now have to find another provider. Today I received another argumentative telephone call from your mother who accused me of inaccurate information in regards to a previously agreed-to payment issue. I can no longer allow this verbal abuse (witnessed by my student) to continue and I believe you will be better served by another provider.

Per your own admission in 2002 you were diagnosed with Type 2 Diabetes Mellitus but had been non compliant with care secondary to not being under a providers care. You stated, "No one would see you." We agreed to work together and you agreed to routine lab work and follow-up care. This week I provided you with a free 90 day supply of your medication via the patient assistance program to include:

* *Zetia 10 mg*
* *Gluctrol XL 10 mg*

- *Caudet 10/40 mg*
- *Actos 30 mg*
- *Lisinopril 10 mg (per Dr. Blank)*

I arranged for you to be seen by a specialist. I also facilitated your bilateral cataract surgery which required much communication with Dr. Blank, his office staff and the Eye Consultants. We discussed the importance of your health care need secondary to the following diagnosis:

- *Diabetes Mellitus*
- *Hypertension*
- *Proteinuria with renal insufficient*
- *Morbid Obesity (> or =350 pounds)*

You may not have understood the depth of care your medical conditions have required, however when you signed the clinic policy form you agreed to medical compliance and payment for services rendered. I faxed completed physicals (two times) with lab work that provided medical clearance for your eye surgery. I wrote two letters to Dr. Blank and faxed lab results to keep all communication open. I have been truly concerned with your medical condition. As you know the clinic is not free, so much of what I have done has been to benefit your health and wellness, but I can no longer accept the verbal assaults made by you and your family.

Best regards,

Anne Boston Parish, MSN, RN, CS; FNP-C

CC: Dr. Blank

PART VIII

Events You Won't Believe

Going to Prison:
What part of "NO" do you not understand?

One day a patient walked into the clinic. He was a returning patient, so he was extremely familiar with the clinic fee policy. What followed was truly amazing. This was his second office visit. It had been four years since his last office visit. The fee for an office visit had been $45, it is now $60. Additionally, he knew that any other procedures, laboratory work or office testing was an additional fee. This patient was familiar with the clinic policy. His chief complaint was that he wanted to stop smoking! At the front desk, prior to being charged, he was told that his concern could be addressed, but it would require a laboratory test called a Liver Function Test (LFT) to which he agreed. The payment is always made prior to the examination. When he came in, he told me what he needed, and agreed to the office visit and the laboratory test (LFT). After he sat down, he spoke about his smoking and how he wanted to stop. The real *objective* of his visit was for a Xanax prescription, a controlled drug, for his anxiety.

He later told me that he had committed a crime, and he was going to the State Prison the next day. I told him, "There are nurses and doctors at the State Prison, and they would attend to your anxiety if they felt you needed medication to be prepared for your sentence." He continued to argue saying that they really didn't care and wouldn't give him the medication. I responded, "That is their decision." I also did not feel comfortable giving him a controlled drug after this admission. I was concerned he may overdose on the medication for his anxiety and have to be admitted to a hospital rather than go to prison. This is competent medical supervision for someone who may alter his health condition rather than fulfill a prison sentence. I was using prudent, safe medical care for someone who was "drug-seeking."

After I refused to write the prescription, he became very hostile and verbally threatened me. He demanded his money back. I told him he had agreed to the charges prior to the office visit and there were no refunds. This is another reason to have a signed merchant slip with the no refund policy printed on the signature copy for the office records. He received an office visit, counseling, and I would have provided a prescription for his original request for smoking cessation. When I offered this plan to him he refused the option and demanded his money back.

I later received a dispute notice from his merchant card service. The dispute stated that he wanted "a refund for medical services and the agreed to laboratory work." The patient declined the options that I provided, which included laboratory work so that I could prescribe the medication he originally had requested. He left Queen Street Clinic yelling and demanding that all his money be returned. He had already agreed to the services that the clinic would offer and clearly understood the clinic policy.

I was amazed that after he was released from prison he pursued receiving a refund. What part of "**NO**" did he not understand? After all, he really wanted a controlled substance so he would be able to tolerate prison more easily. Not only is this unrealistic, but it is my understanding that when one goes to prison it is for a crime committed and not a holiday or vacation. His request was not only inappropriate, but it would have been unethical to prescribe him a controlled substance. Sometimes "NO" is not the word a patient wants to hear. My policy has always been to provide safe and prudent care, and when I sense a patient is drug-seeking I am not willing to compromise this standard. Additionally, my clinic is not free. I always encourage all patients to read the clinic policy before agreeing to the services. After receiving care and service, I expect to be paid by the merchant account for the agreed-upon care.

Shortly after, I replied to the bank sponsoring his credit card and provided a copy of the signed merchant slip. A reversal of charges was granted and the money was reinstated to my merchant account.

The Gift of a Free Infant

One day a young lady walked into the clinic with a two-week-old infant girl. She stated she was the guardian of the infant and claimed the child was given to her. I asked her to produce the delivery room paperwork or an affidavit to support this claim. When I inquired where the child was born, she replied, "In Washington State." I asked her why she was not using the Public Health Department. She replied she did not want the Commonwealth of Virginia's involvement with the infant's health care. For that reason she came to this clinic. At that moment, the "red flag" went up in my mind. The Queen Street Clinic is in Virginia. There was no paperwork to support and identify this young lady as the legal guardian. It was alarming no paperwork was in her possession to confirm her legal custody of the infant. She continued to say the infant's father was her husband.

I asked her permission to call the police and seek their assistance so that the infant would be registered in the public health system for medical care. At that suggestion, the young woman picked up the infant and ran out of the clinic. I called 911 and followed her out of the clinic to write down her car's license plate.

The Alexandria and Fairfax police departments later found the infant's location by tracking down the license plate number and confirming some of the information that had been presented to me. The police requested that the biological father and mother, who were still in the state of Washington, deliver an overnight legal document to verify legal custody of the infant.

The infant was in the custody of someone who did not have adequate paperwork to support her claim on the child. When I later spoke to the police, they expressed their appreciation for my quick response in light of so many kidnappings and incidences of child abuse.

No Smoking

One day as I was treating a patient, a former patient walked in without an appointment. I told her four other people were ahead of her in line. This was fine with her, but she insisted that I give her a specific time for an appointment. This type of request is not unusual. I told her to return in one hour. That was just a guess. I returned to my patient and before I knew it, the woman's husband exploded through the screened door of the patient triage area to use the restroom. This took me by surprise. I told him I was in the middle of seeing a patient and must wait or use a restroom down the street. He was fine with this and walked away, but not before he lit his cigarette from a lighted scented candle on the counter. I did not notice he was smoking a cigarette until another patient screamed, "This man is smoking in the lobby!" I immediately asked him what he was doing and why would he light a cigarette in the clinic. He did not respond but slowly sauntered toward the door.

Within a few minutes, a heated argument erupted between the patient who informed me about the smoking and the patient who was waiting to be seen. One patient challenged the other patient to step outside where she would "take care of her."

I do not believe there was anything I could have done to diffuse this confrontation. In fact, when I asked that the patient's husband step out of the clinic with the lit cigarette, his wife became very angry at me for asking him to leave the clinic. Part of the argument involved one of my patients telling the other patient to be more respectful of me, my medical practice and the other patients sitting in the lobby. Who would have ever guessed someone would light a cigarette in the clinic? My Clinic Rules now include "No Smoking in the Clinic!"

CONCLUSION

Sometimes I wish I could look into a crystal ball and predict who will provide the necessary health care for our working poor. I know that I have offered my community one option for the delivery of its health care. I am hopeful that by reading this book, you too will take the challenge and emulate the building of a medical home similar to the Queen Street Clinic.

What lies ahead for those who are medically uninsured? Will those individuals who are forced into early retirement or buy-outs be able to find a medical insurance policy to adequately take care of their health care needs? Daily I hear national news reports of major companies offering their employees incentives for early retirements and buy-outs. In essence, this is a means to increase the company's profits and decrease overhead. Many of these incentive offers do not include the individual's ongoing health care coverage. Recently, I heard of an incentive offer of $35,000 for one corporation's employees to voluntarily leave their job and take an early retirement or buy-out. Despite this large lump-sum amount, one affected person said that the dollar amount was not enough of a financial incentive to adequately continue their health care coverage at its current level. This is especially true if an unforeseen health care need turns into a chronic illness.

Similar to the growth of a tree from a seed, I was able to see in a run-down store front the potential for growing a derelict structure into a productive home of hope and health for the medically uninsured — my future patients. With fresh paint and considerable elbow grease, 1000 Queen Street could be transformed into a refuge for those who did not have a medical home. My passion has always been the delivery of health care, and my dedication has been to those less fortunate. Much of my strength has come from the faith in my ability to see an opportunity and then see it through to fruition. At times the cause seemed larger than me. The odds were not in my favor for this venture to succeed. But the importance of my goal compelled me to keep focused. I kept my eye on the prize, so to speak; the prize being to design a medical model of health care that did not rely on the not-for-profit world to support a patient population without health care insurance. I wanted to give ownership for health care back to the patient who was medically uninsured. I know today that need is still there because every day I treat uninsured individuals who are willing to pay an affordable fee for competent medical care.

As I reflect on the care provided over the last few years, I think of those who are now able to remain healthy by receiving preventative care. I am proud to have met the challenge and overcome the obstacles. Few believed I could build a clinic for our community's working poor, but after seven years, my success is evident. More than

20,000 patients have received care, and the clinic has a 60 percent patient following. This means 60 percent of patients receiving care at the Queen Street Clinic consider it their medical home and now seek care in the clinic instead of the hospital emergency room.

Writing this book has been a humbling experience. It is my sincere hope that you will come away with a better appreciation of the challenges that face our medically uninsured. Within the pages of this book, I have outlined one path to support building community clinics that do not rely on local, state or federal funding for our 47 million medically uninsured Americans. Referencing the December 2007 release of a federal report on health care, the director of the U.S. Centers for Disease Control and Prevention, Dr. Julie Gerberding, claimed that access to health care is still an issue where we need improvement, even though there has been significant progress made in the areas of health and life expectancy.*

I think leaders inspire us. I do not consider myself unique. When I look around at what I have been able to accomplish and the lives I have touched, maybe I understate my ability to be a leader in my community and a medical pioneer. I believe I have been a champion for those who have never had an advocate to fight for their interests and manage their medical care.

My sincere hope is that more clinics will be built to help those who are medically uninsured. Metaphorically speaking, you will be

---

* Maggie Fox, "Over 40 million in U.S. can't afford health care: report," REUTERS, December 3, 2007. http://www.reuters.com/ articleId=USN0343703420071203. See www.cdc.gov/nchs/

building "castles in the sky" for those without health care to use as a safe haven for their health care needs. I trust that others will join my efforts to replicate the building blocks of the Queen Street Clinic so the 47 million medically uninsured Americans may be privileged to receive the health care they so desperately need and deserve.

One final note — daily I am often encouraged by the patients who write letters of gratitude for my efforts, devotion, and personal funds that built the Queen Street Clinic. I am frequently reminded that I am the clinic; so in many ways my spirit, personality, and dedication come through as I deliver health care. I am hopeful you will be inspired by my words to follow your dreams. Good luck, and remember — nothing of value ever comes easy!

APPENDIX

City of Alexandria, Virginia
301 King Street, Suite 2300
Alexandria, Virginia 22314

Kerry J. Donley
Mayor

(703) 838-4500
Fax (703) 838-6433

July 13, 2000

Ms. Anne Parish
230 North St. Asaph Street
Alexandria, VA 22314

Dear Anne:

I have reviewed your proposal for a medical office to be located in the City of Alexandria and I am supportive of the concept and your plans. This office would provide medical services to those not presently served by public facilities and insurance companies. Such an office could have tremendous benefits to Alexandrians, particularly those seeking preventive health care, thus potentially reducing more costly services as overall health declines and expensive services become necessary. I know you are acutely aware of the burdens placed on hospitals throughout the country, and sites focused on preventive services should be welcomed as true community assets.

Additionally, I understand the zoning in the Inner City section of Alexandria would permit your office to be sited in the CL (commercial low) zone. Thus, from a land use perspective the description of your business is allowable.

I hope you are successful in your endeavors to open this office which would serve Alexandrians in the Inner City area. I welcome you and your business to Alexandria, and I offer my best wishes as you pursue its opening.

Sincerely,

Kerry J. Donley
Mayor

"Home Town of George Washington and Robert E. Lee"

Letter from City of Alexandria: Former Mayor Kerry Donley

City of Alexandria, Virginia

DEPARTMENT OF PLANNING AND ZONING
301 King Street, Room 2100
Alexandria, Virginia   22314
(703) 838-4666
FAX (703) 838-6393

May 3, 2000

Anne Boston Parish
230 North St. Asaph Street
Alexandria, Virginia 22314

Dear Ms. Parish:

In response to your letter dated May 1, 2000, this office has determined from the description of your business operation that you are a medical office and not a medical care facility.

The property located at 1000 Queen Street, Alexandria, Virginia, is zoned CL, commercial low, which permits medical offices. For your information I have enclosed zoning map #64.03 with the subject property highlighted in yellow and the CL zone regulations.

If you have any questions regarding the CL zone, please call me at (703) 838-4688.

Sincerely,

Peter Leiberg
Principal Planner

Attachments: Map #64.03
              CL zone regulations

cc: Sheldon Lynn, Director, Planning Dept

File: P:\Zoning\Corres\2000\1000Qu

Letter from City of Alexandria: Department of Planning and Zoning

Frequently Asked Questions

IS THIS A FREE CLINIC?

No, this is a clinic for the medically uninsured. We don't accept insurance, Medicaid/Medicare.

I HAVE TO PAY FIRST? WILL YOU TAKE A CHECK?

Yes, you must pay before you receive care. We don't take checks or have a payment plan. Cash, MasterCard or VISA are the only acceptable forms of payment.

I GET THIS ILLNESS EVERY YEAR; I DON'T WANT TO PAY FOR THE OFFICE VISIT. I JUST NEED ANTIBIOTICS.

There are now antibiotic resistant "bugs" due to provider overuse. Specific body systems require specific antibiotics. We are credentialed professionals who determine through a focused physical exam and many times lab tests (e.g., throat culture, urine dip or blood work) a working diagnosis required for distribution of antibiotics.

I JUST LOST MY INSURANCE AND HAVE A CHRONIC ILLNESS DIAGNOSED BY MY PREVIOUS PROVIDER. I DON'T WANT TO PAY FOR LAB WORK. I JUST WANT MY MEDICATIONS REFILLED.

Unless you have your entire medical file with all your information regarding your chronic illness (e.g., diabetes, COPD, depression, etc.) with blood work results within the last two weeks, we can't just give you medicine. In order to practice GOOD medicine we are required to perform a complete history and physical, as well as laboratory work to properly decide if the medication you are currently on is working. We are required to ensure your organs (i.e., kidney and/or liver) are in good health in order to continue or increase medications. Many times we need to run specific labs to confirm your diagnosis.

I THOUGHT YOU HELPED THE POOR.

This is not a free clinic, nor is it a non-profit organization. Queen Street Clinic Clinic does not receive additional money from the state or federal government for subsidized operating expenses in order to keep its doors open. We do provide discounted health care (refer to the pricing sheet). If you went to an urgent care facility in the immediate Alexandria area you would pay on average $110.00 just to walk in the door, and that does not include any lab tests, x-rays, or in-clinic treatments. The ER is almost double that.

DO YOU PROVIDE IMMUNIZATION SERVICES?

Queen Street only performs TB skin tests and tetanus and flu shots.

DOES ANYONE HERE SPEAK SPANISH?

Yes, the owner and sole provider speaks Spanish.

I QUALIFY FOR A MEDICATION ASSISTANCE PROGRAM, SO WHY DO I HAVE TO PAY FOR PERIODIC LAB TESTS?

We would be practicing poor health care if we were not performing required regular lab tests to ensure that specific internal organs are kept healthy and that your medications are working properly. They may periodically need adjusting.

WHY DO I HAVE TO PAY FOR AN OFFICE VISIT FOR ABNORMAL LAB RESULTS?

Abnormal results require patient education about this "newly found" information and how these results affect your future health. Many times patients will require new medications and/or multiple new medications over time. All patients require an understanding of what their future care will entail with any new diagnosis.

I LOST MY PRESCRIPTION. WHY DO I HAVE TO PAY FOR A NEW WRITTEN PRESCRIPTION?

We are accountable for every prescription that "walks out" this door. The medical provider's professional oath obliges him/her to ensure the patient doesn't misuse the prescription.

All of us who give service, and stand ready for sacrifice, are torch bearers. We run with the torches until we fall, content if we can pass them to the hands of some other runners... both life and death are parts of the same adventure.

— Theodore Roosevelt

OWNER, FOUNDER AND CONSULTANT

Anne Boston Parish is a Family Nurse Practitioner who resides in Alexandria, Virginia. Anne is a graduate of Marymount University in Arlington, Virginia. After raising her children, she used her personal funds to build a clinic for the medically uninsured. Anne has made a considerable contribution to her community for the medically uninsured. She was named in 2002 as a *Washingtonian Award* recipient. Anne has been featured in local and national newspapers, as well as in nursing journals, including:

Photography by Tisara INC (Nina Tisara)

- The Washington Post
- Old Town Crier
- Alexandria Gazette Packet and The Alexandria Journal
- The Alexandria Chamber of Commerce, Chamber Currents
- Nursing Spectrum
- Nurse Practitioner World News
- Advance for Nurses and the American Journal of Nursing
- MU Today, The Magazine for Marymount University
- Alexandria Times
- Del Ray Sun

Washington D.C.'s ABC affiliate, Channel 7 News and Toyota honored her by presenting her with *A Tribute to the Working Women Award* in 2004. CNN and ABC affiliate Channel 7 News in Washington, DC, have also interviewed her. Both Anne and the clinic have received much praise from both her peers and various organizations. The Queen Street Clinic was featured in a DVD for the annual conference of the American Academy of Nurse Practitioners in July 2005. Additionally, Anne has consulted for a number of organizations, including a teleconference with VHA in Irving, Texas, to implement a community-based clinic for the medically-uninsured, and a national consumer-focused healthcare company that was building walk-in clinics in supermarkets. She is on the faculty of local universities and has been published in various nursing journals.

In 2007 Anne was nominated to receive a *Living Legend Award* for the difference she has made in the Alexandria Community. The Queen Street Clinic is able to provide health care to those less fortunate and who are medically uninsured. In addition to working as the sole medical provider at the Queen Street Clinic, Anne is available for consultation either for long-term projects or short-term profiles.

Anne Boston Parish, MSN, CS; RN; FNP-C
Family Nurse Practitioner
Founder and Owner
Queen Street Clinic, PLC
1000 Queen Street
Alexandria, Virginia 22314
703-299-9701 (office)
703-299-9701 (fax)
www.queenstreetclinic.com

SELECTED BIOGRAPHICAL NOTES

Robert Byrne (b.1930), Author and billiards champion player.

Winston Churchill (1874-1965), British politician, Former Prime Minister of United Kingdom, statesman, orator, strategist, author, British army officer.

John J. Collins Jr. M.D., VHA Inc. Sr. Vice President, Clinical Affairs (2001).

Ralph Waldo Emerson (1803-1882), Unitarian minister, writer, and speaker. American's best known and best loved 19 century figure.

Benjamin Franklin (1706-1790), Committee member that drafted the Declaration of Independence, printer, publisher, author, discovered electricity.

Victor Hugo (1802-1885), Famous French poet, playwright, novelist, essayist.

C. Everett Koop (b 1916), MD, former Surgeon General.

Mary Lyon (1797-1849), Founder of the Mount Holyoke Female Seminary and a pioneer in women's education in America.

James Earl Parker (b.1948), Friend and patient of the Queen Street Clinic, a cancer survivor and fine gentlemen.

Eleanor Roosevelt (1884-1961), One of the most well-known and admired first ladies, wife of Franklin Delano Roosevelt.

Theodore Roosevelt (1858-1919), Twenty-sixth president of the United States, Nobel Peace Prize awarded in 1906.

CPSIA information can be obtained at www.ICGtesting.com
Printed in the USA
LVOW05s1700180713

343558LV00008B/889/P

9 781434 360168